Guitar Scale Book

Guitar Command

www.GuitarCommand.com

By Laurence Harwood.

Edited by Dan Wright.

Published by Timescale Music

ISBN: 978-0-9556566-5-1

This publication Copyright © 2014 by L. Harwood. All Rights Reserved. This publication may not be copied or distributed in whole or in part without prior written permission from the copyright holder.

Contents

Introduction 4

Guitar Scales 5

How To Read Guitar Scale Diagrams 5

Scale Spellings 6

Guitar Fretboard Diagram 7

   Major Scale / Ionian Modal Scale 8

   Pentatonic Minor Scale 9

   Pentatonic Major Scale 10

   Blues Scale 11

   Dorian Modal Scale 12

   Phrygian Modal Scale 13

   Lydian Modal Scale 14

   Mixolydian Modal Scale 15

   Aeolian Modal Scale / Natural Minor Scale 16

   Locrian Modal Scale 17

   Harmonic Minor Scale 18

   Jazz Minor Scale / Melodic Minor Scale 19

   Phrygian Dominant Scale 20

   Double Harmonic Scale 21

   Persian Scale 22

   Neapolitan Minor Scale 23

   Neapolitan Major Scale 24

   Bebop Dominant Scale 25

   Bebop Minor Scale 26

   Bebop Major Scale 27

Altered Scale 28

Lydian Augmented Scale 29

Mixolydian #4 / Lydian ♭7 Scale 30

Locrian #2 Scale 31

Diminished Scale 32

Whole Tone Scale 34

Chromatic Scale 35

Japanese Scales 36

In Scale 36

Hirajoshi 36

Yo Scale 37

Arpeggios 38

Major 38

Minor 39

Dominant 7th 39

Minor 7th 40

Major 7th 40

Major Add 9 41

Minor Add 9 41

Diminished 7th 42

Minor 7th Flat 5 42

Dominant 9th 43

Dominant 11th 43

Dominant 13th 44

Minor 9th 44

Minor 11th 45

Minor 13th 45

Introduction

The *Guitar Scale Book* contains a comprehensive collection of guitar scales for use in all styles of music. You can work through the book from beginning to end to improve your knowledge of scales, or use it to find specific information quickly and easily.

This book is aimed at guitarists who use scales and arpeggios in improvisation. It is suitable for electric and acoustic guitarists of all styles and abilities.

Having a good knowledge of scales and arpeggios is beneficial whatever kind of music you play.

The scales and arpeggios in this book are presented in diagram form; you do not have to read music to use the book. Notation and tab have been provided in addition to the fretboard diagrams. This allows guitarists to compare how the fretboard diagrams relate to the actual musical notation. The scales and arpeggios are notated with a root note of C.

The diagrams show movable shapes. This means that, using just one shape, a scale or arpeggio can be played with any root note. Multiple shapes are provided, allowing the whole of the fretboard to be utilized. This approach reflects how most guitarists learn and use scales and arpeggios.

We hope that you enjoy using this book and that your playing benefits from the information it contains.

Guitar Command

Guitar Command is a website and specialist guitar publisher.

Visit **www.GuitarCommand.com** for guitar news, information and free lessons. Improve your lead guitar playing with **Guitar Command Backing Track** albums, available to download from online stores.

Also Available

Guitar Chord Book

A comprehensive resource for guitarists. Contains hundreds of guitar chord diagrams for use in any kind of music.

ISBN: 978-0-9556566-4-4

Guitar Chords, Scales & Arpeggios: The Complete Guitar Reference Book

The complete reference book for all guitarists. Contains all of the information from the Guitar Chord Book and the Guitar Scale Book in one volume.

ISBN: 978-0-9556566-6-8

Guitar Scales

This book contains guitar scales that can be used in improvisation and composition. Each scale is presented in diagram form and in notation with tab. Information on each scale is also provided.

The scale diagrams show the notes of the scale in relation to the tonic note (the tonic note is the note from which the scale is formed, i.e. the C of a C major scale).

Multiple diagrams are provided for each scale, allowing the scale to be played in different fretboard positions.

Combine two or more scale diagrams (by changing fretboard position as you play) to create multi-octave scales and longer lines.

How To Read Guitar Scale Diagrams

Scale diagrams represent the guitar fretboard. They show where the fretting fingers should be placed in order to play a scale.

The tonic notes of the scale are represented by white circles; the black circles show all of the other notes in the scale that are available at that position.

The diagram below shows how a major scale diagram is used to play a G major scale.

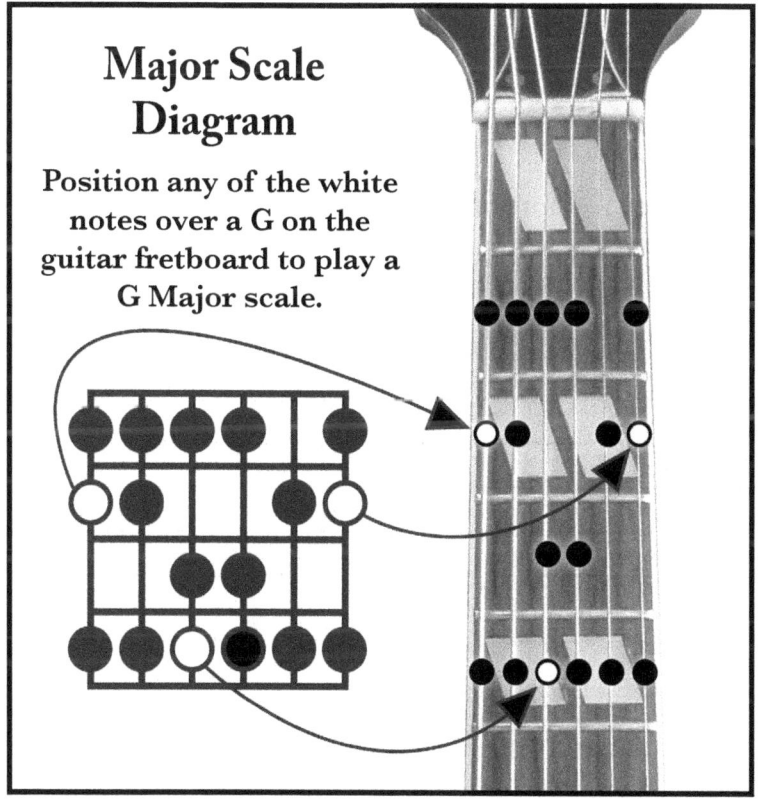

Major Scale Diagram

Position any of the white notes over a G on the guitar fretboard to play a G Major scale.

In this example the white circles (representing the root notes of the scale) are positioned over G notes on the fretboard.

The scale produced by playing up from one white note to another is a G major scale.

If you were to position your hand so that the white circles were over A notes on the fretboard, the same shape would produce an A major scale.

If necessary, use the guitar fretboard diagram on page 7 to position the white notes over the tonic note you need.

Notes On Reading Scale Diagrams

- *Start and finish on white notes to play a scale; play to the first white note for a one octave scale; play to the second for a two octave scale (for shapes that have three white notes).*

- *Combine scale diagrams to play multi-octave scales and longer lines.*

- *All of the notes (black and white) can be used in improvisation.*

- *Use the guitar fretboard diagram on page 7 to correctly position movable scale shapes.*

When playing just the scale, start and end on white notes. Play up to the top note then play back down the scale to the starting note. The top note is usually only played once.

When using the scale in improvisation, all of the notes (black and white) can be used. (While improvising, you would not necessarily play the notes in the scale sequentially, therefore the diagrams show **all** of the notes in the scale available in that position on the fretboard.)

Some scale diagrams can be used for more than one tonic note (e.g. diminished scale diagrams). Where this occurs, all of the potential tonic / root notes are shown as white circles.

Scale Spellings

Scale spellings show the notes of a scale compared to those of a major scale. They are useful for learning and comparing scales.

Examples of scale spellings are shown in the chart below:

Scale Type	Scale Spelling	Notes With Tonic Of C
Major	1, 2, 3, 4, 5, 6, 7	C, D, E, F, G, A, B
Dorian	1, 2, ♭3, 4, 5, 6, ♭7	C, D, E♭, F, G, A, B♭
Phrygian	1, 2, 3, ♯4, 5, 6, 7	C, D, E, F♯, G, A, B

Guitar Fretboard Diagram

Use the guitar fretboard diagram below to correctly position movable scale and arpeggio shapes. Standard string numbering is used, from 6 (the low E string) to 1 (the high E string).

The shaded areas on the diagram represent the frets which, on most guitars, contain dots or other inlaid markers.

String

Fret Number	6	5	4	3	2	1
Open	E	A	D	G	B	E
1	F	A#/Bb	D#/Eb	G#/Ab	C	F
2	F#/Gb	B	E	A	C#/Db	F#/Gb
3	G	C	F	A#/Bb	D	G
4	G#/Ab	C#/Db	F#/Gb	B	D#/Eb	G#/Ab
5	A	D	G	C	E	A
6	A#/Bb	D#/Eb	G#/Ab	C#/Db	F	A#/Bb
7	B	E	A	D	F#/Gb	B
8	C	F	A#/Bb	D#/Eb	G	C
9	C#/Db	F#/Gb	B	E	G#/Ab	C#/Db
10	D	G	C	F	A	D
11	D#/Eb	G#/Ab	C#/Db	F#/Gb	A#/Bb	D#/Eb
12	E	A	D	G	B	E

(At the 12th fret, notes are repeated an octave higher.)

Major Scale / Ionian Modal Scale

The 'standard', familiar sounding scale, upon which the scale spelling system is based. Many famous melodies have been written using the major scale, and it is also commonly used in improvisation. Major scales can also be referred to as Ionian modal scales.

Scale spelling: 1, 2, 3, 4, 5, 6, 7

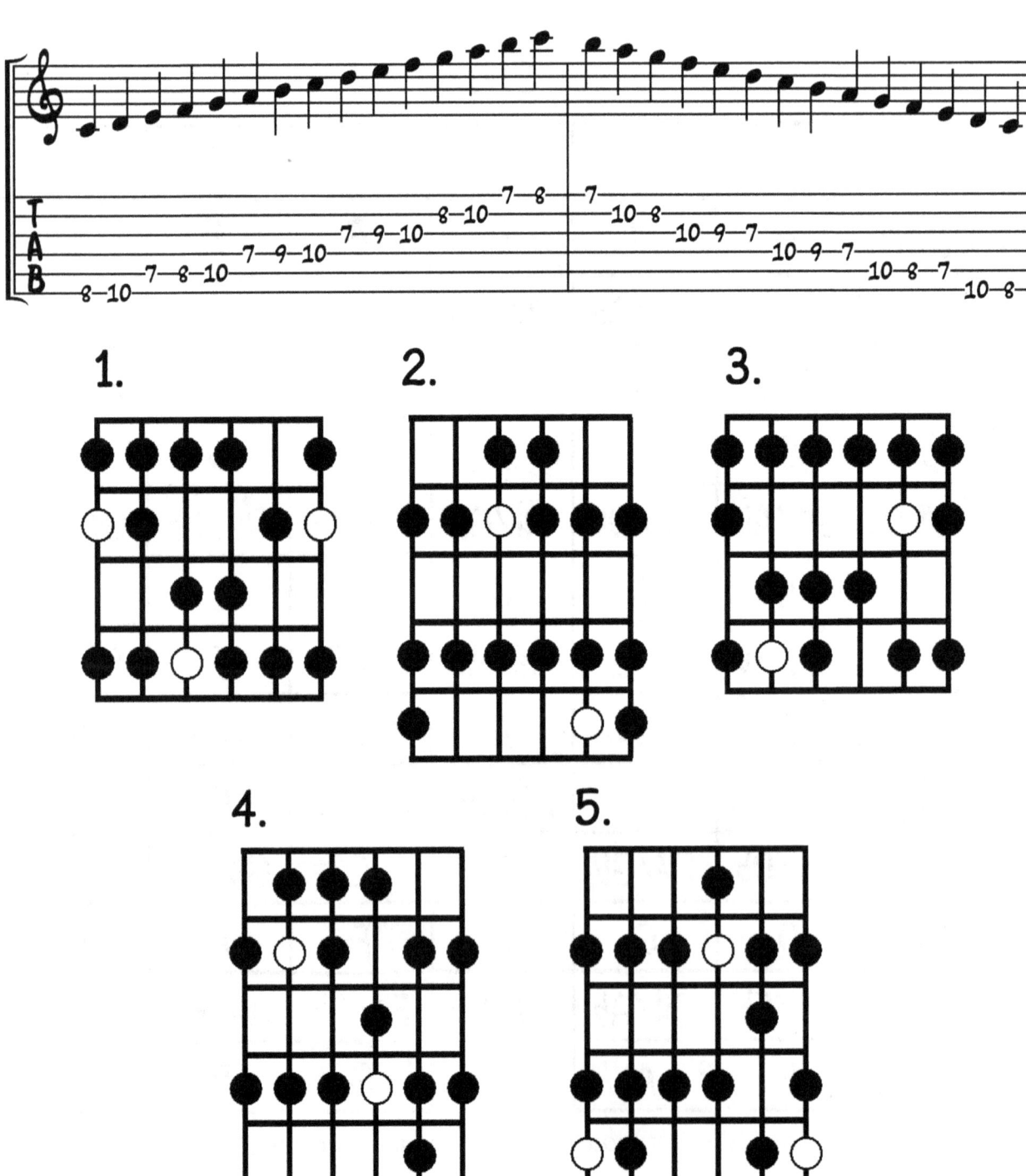

Pentatonic Minor Scale

The pentatonic minor scale forms the basis of many famous guitar solos and riffs. It is used by practically every lead guitarist in every musical style, and should be among the first guitar scales a beginner guitarist learns.

Scale spelling: 1, ♭3, 4, 5, ♭7

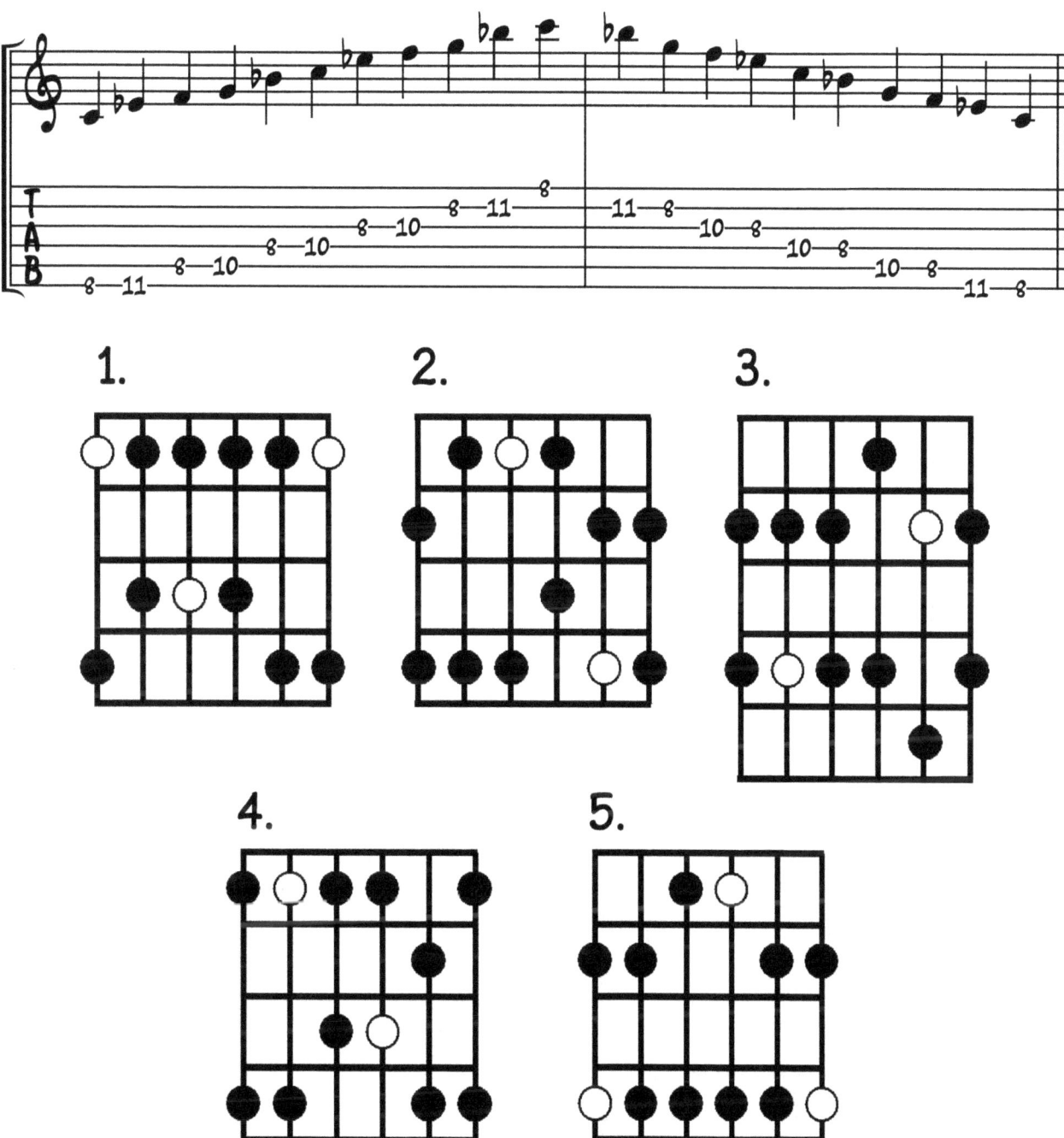

Pentatonic Major Scale

A widely used guitar scale which produces a clear, melodic sound. Ideal for soloing over major chord sequences. Often used in country and rock music. Notice that the shapes are the same as those of the pentatonic minor, but that the root notes are in different positions.

Scale Spelling: 1, 2, 3, 5, 6

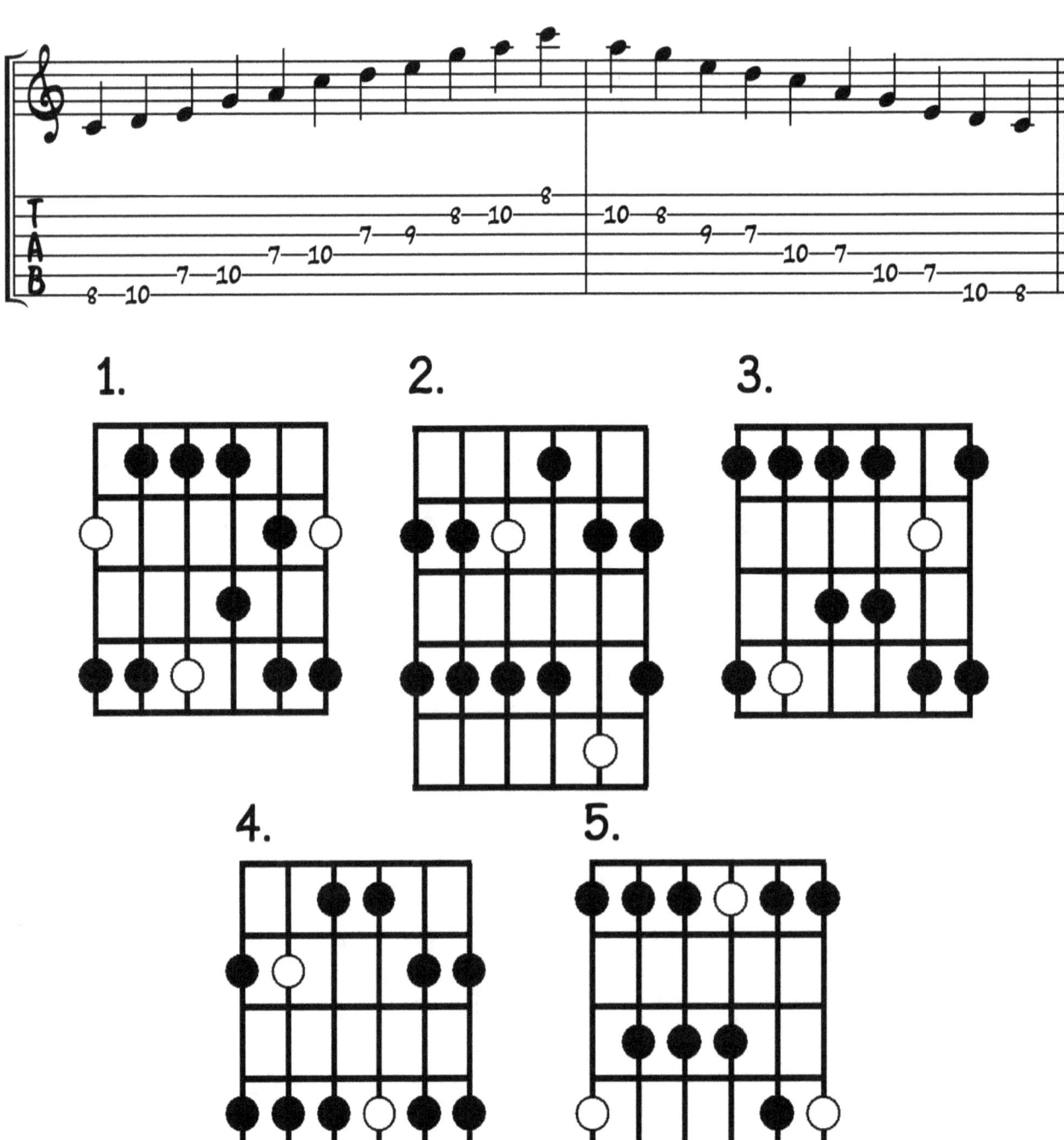

Blues Scale

One of the most frequently used lead guitar scales, and not just in blues music. The blues scale is the same scale as a pentatonic minor, but with an additional note – the flattened fifth. This is known as the 'blues' note, and produces the characteristic blues sound.

Scale spelling: 1, b3, 4, b5, 5, b7

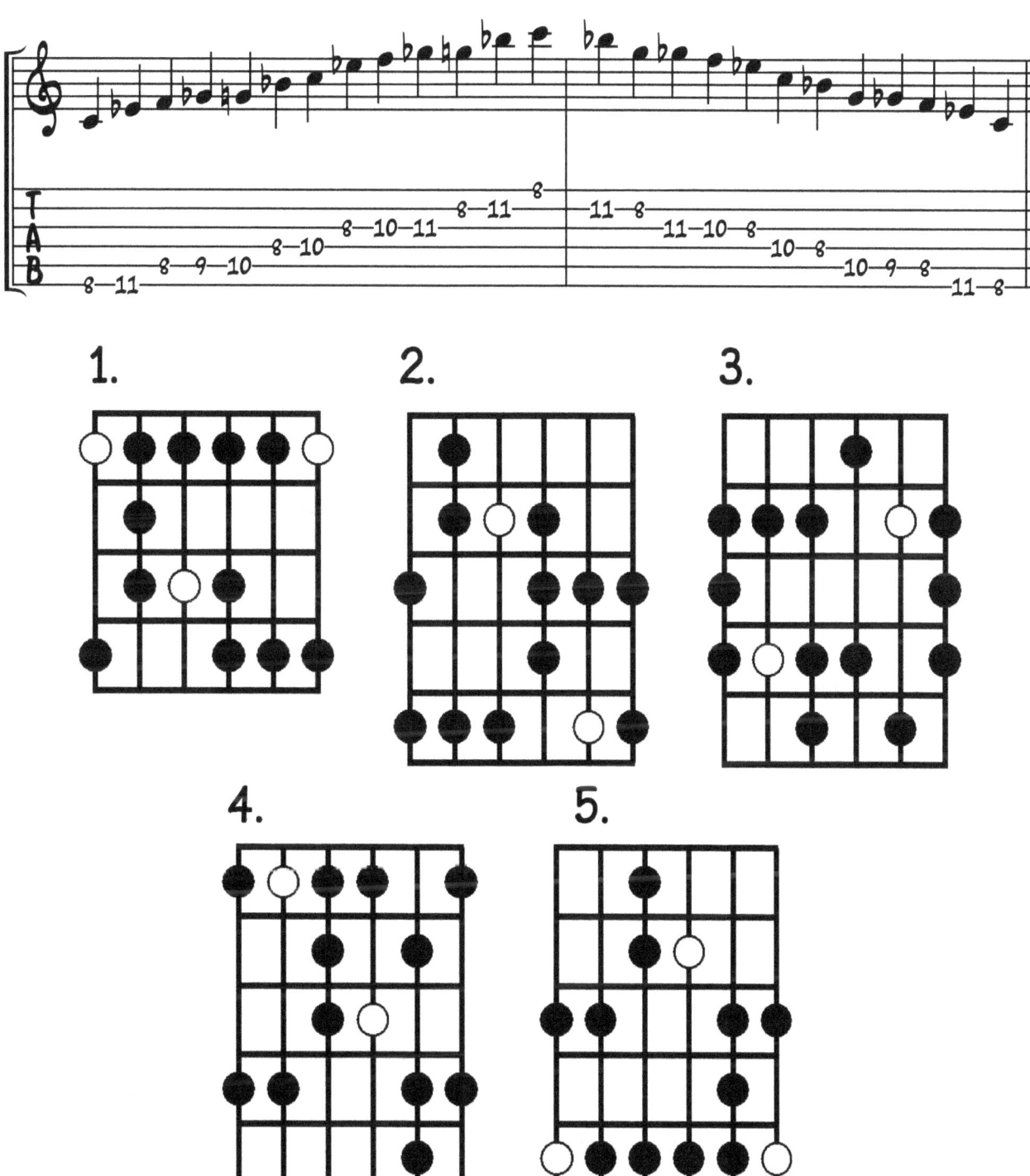

Dorian Modal Scale

The Dorian mode is the second mode of a major scale. It has a distinctive minor tonality and is often used when improvising over minor seventh chords.

Scale spelling: 1, 2, ♭3, 4, 5, 6, ♭7

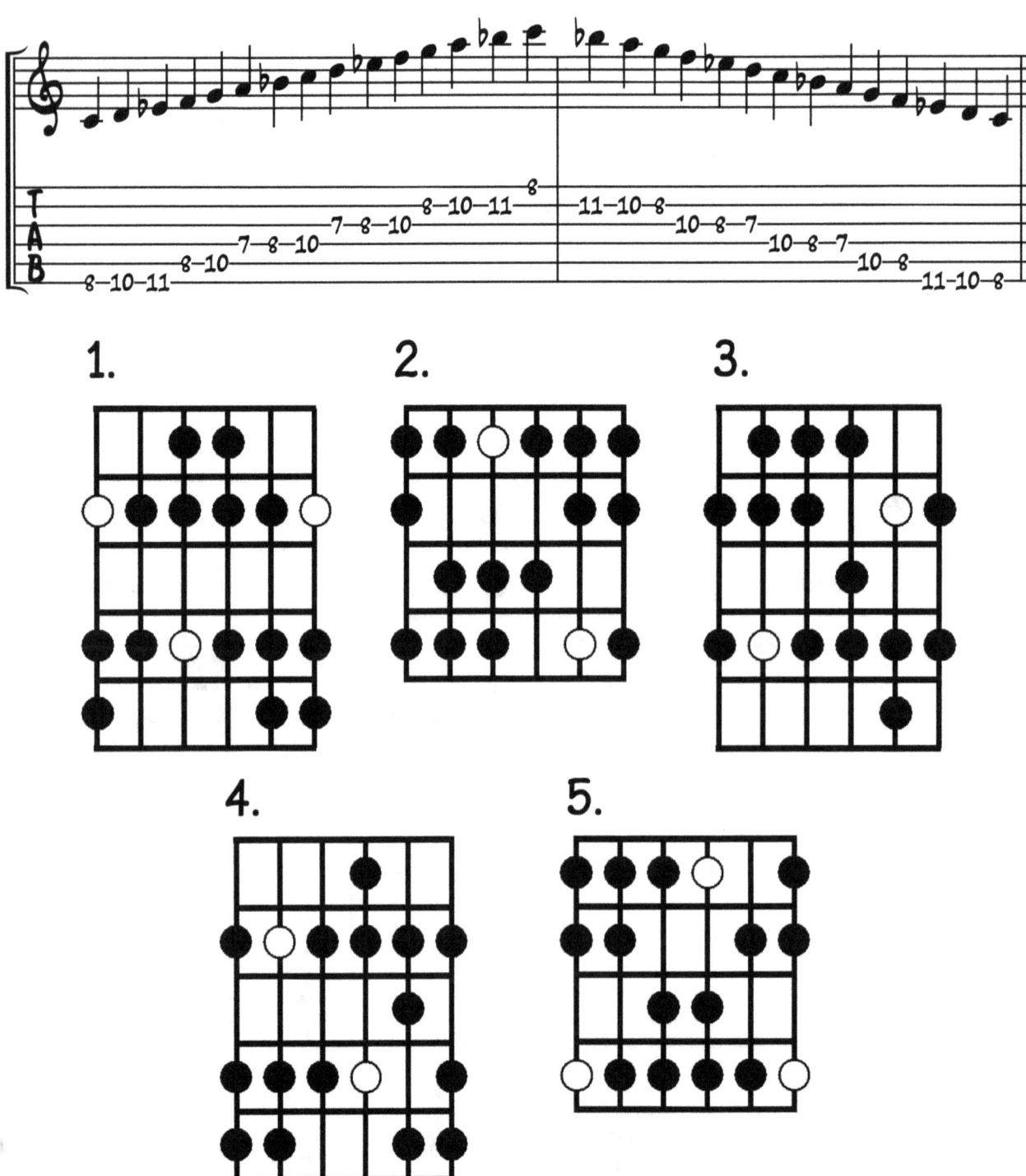

Phrygian Modal Scale

The Phrygian mode is the third mode of a major scale. It is a minor scale, with a slightly 'Eastern' or Spanish sound. It is often used by rock guitarists for soloing over power chords.

Scale spelling: 1, ♭2, ♭3, 4, 5, ♭6, ♭7

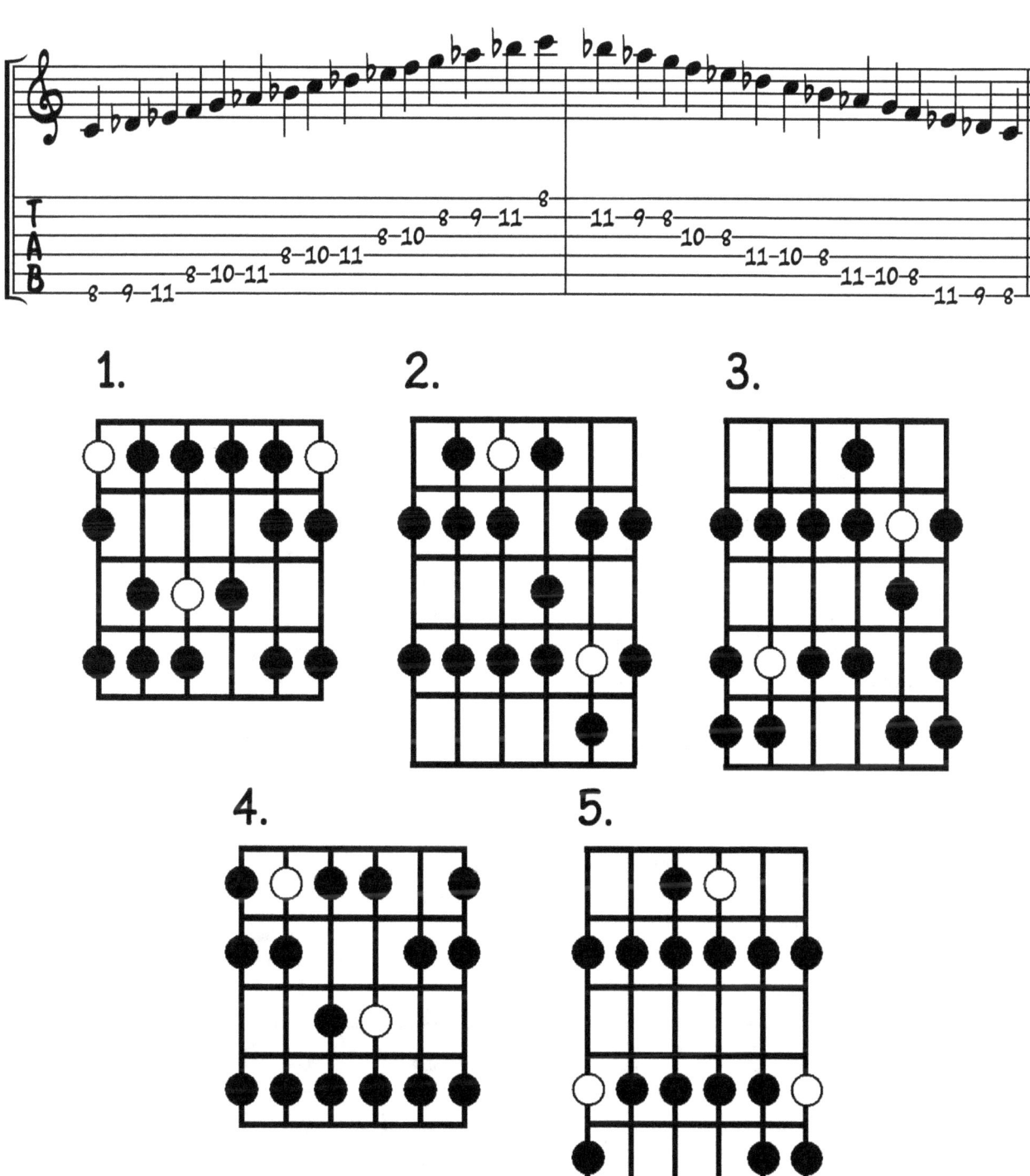

Lydian Modal Scale

The Lydian mode is the fourth mode of a major scale. It is the same as a normal major scale but with a raised fourth note; this forms a tritone (augmented fourth interval) with the tonic note, giving the scale its unique sound.

Scale spelling: 1, 2, 3, ♯4, 5, 6, 7

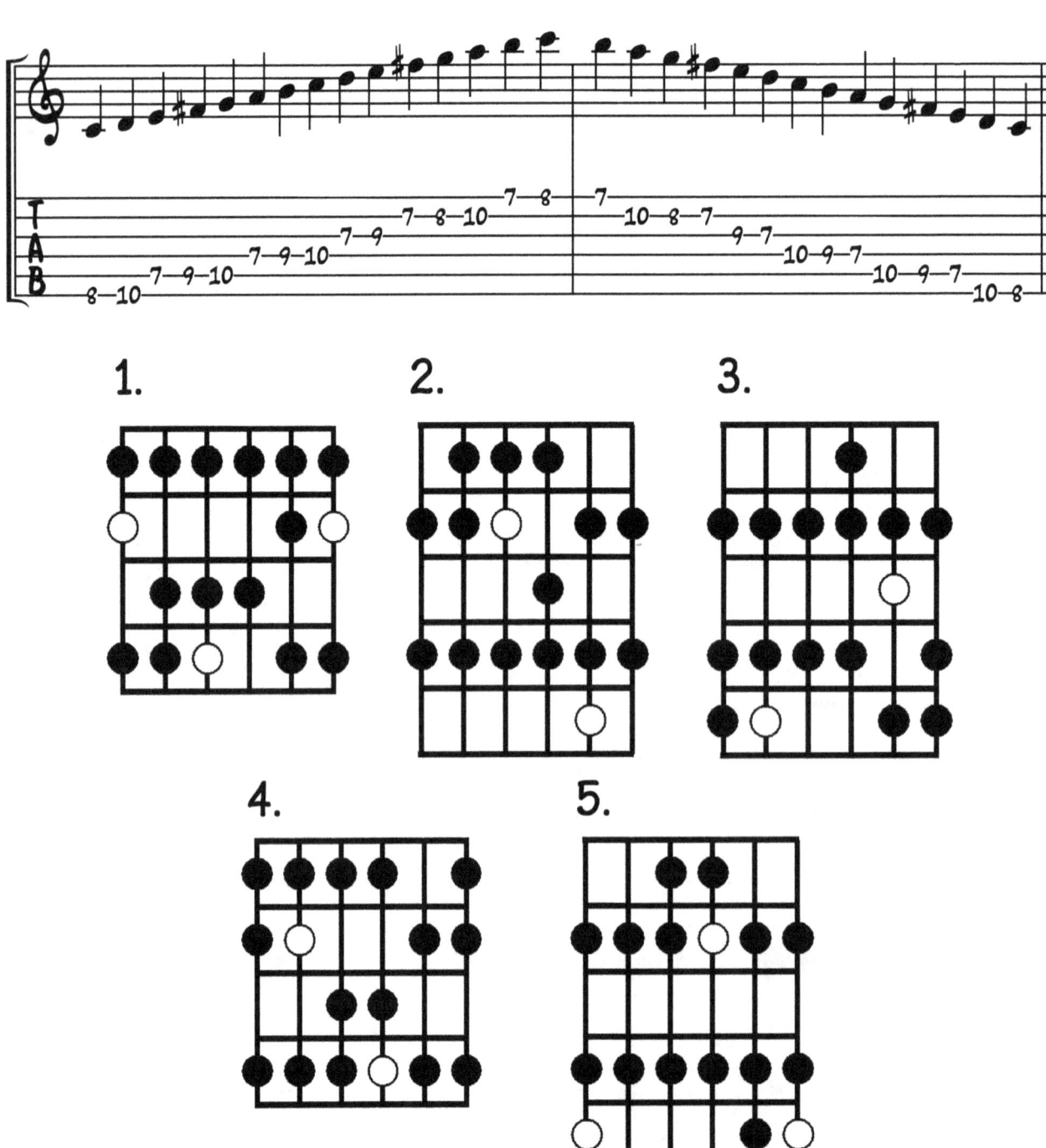

Mixolydian Modal Scale

The Mixolydian mode is the fifth mode of a major scale. Its minor (flattened) seventh note makes it suitable for playing over dominant seventh chords whose root is the same as the tonic note of the scale.

Scale spelling: 1, 2, 3, 4, 5, 6, ♭7

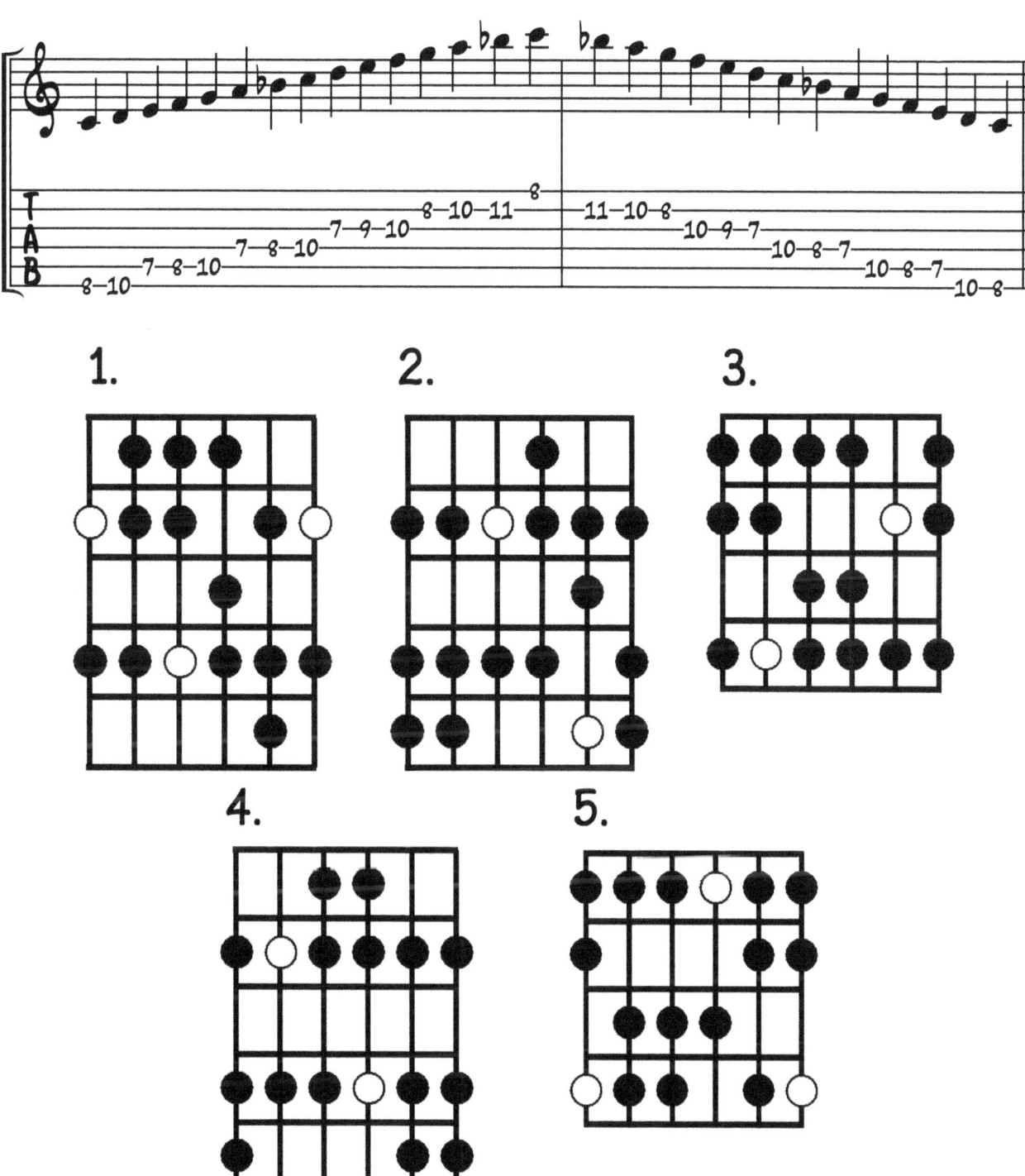

Aeolian Modal Scale / Natural Minor Scale

The Aeolian mode is the sixth mode of a major scale. It is also known as the natural minor scale and can be used to solo over minor chord sequences.

Scale spelling: 1, 2, ♭3, 4, 5, ♭6, ♭7

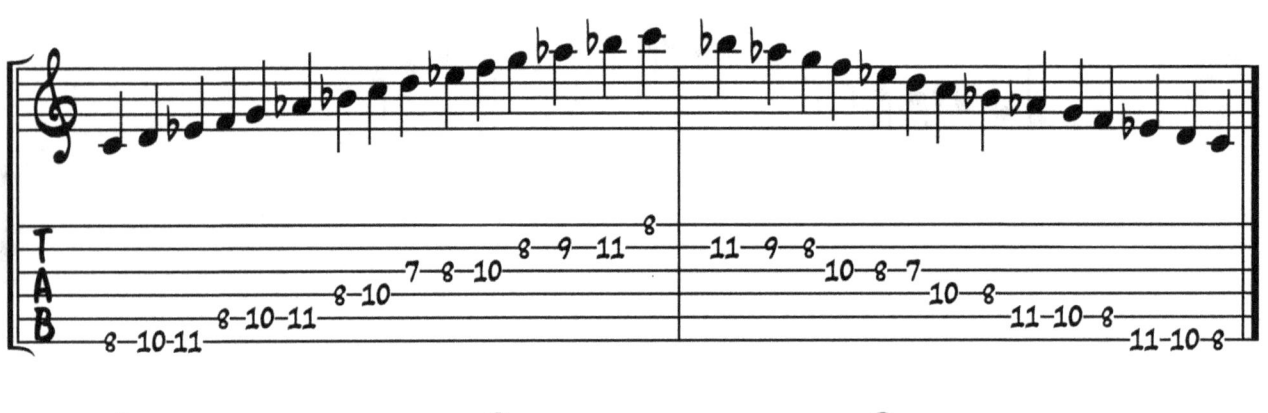

1.

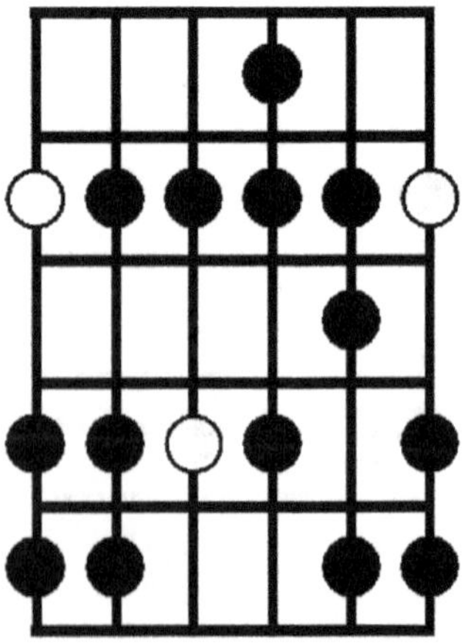

2.

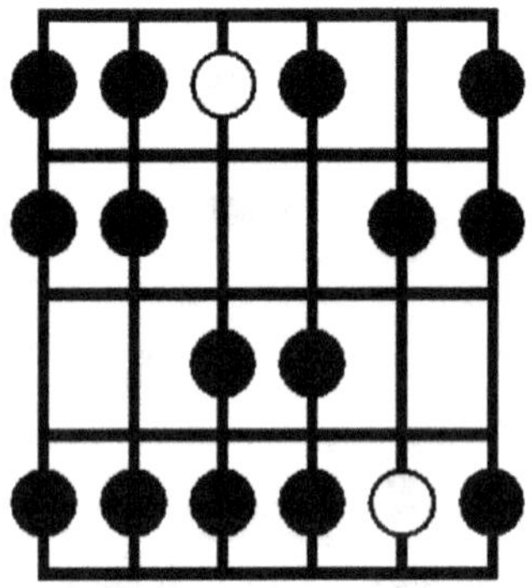

3.

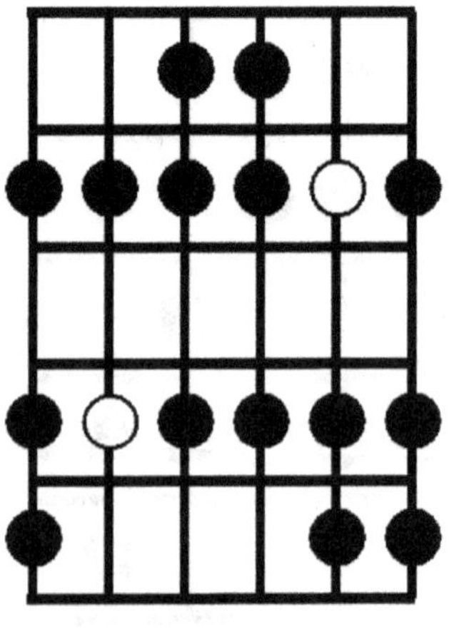

4.

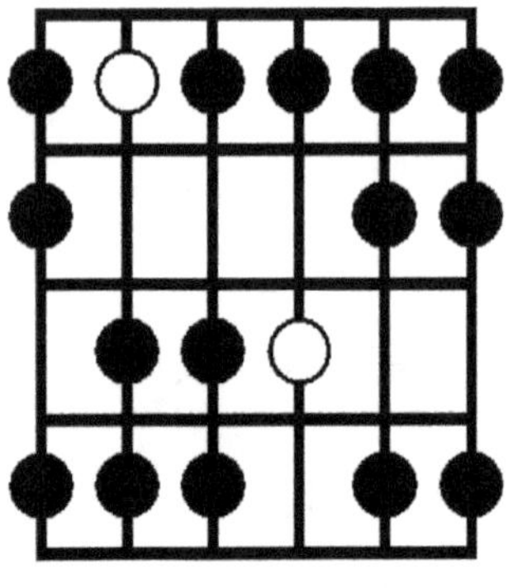

5.

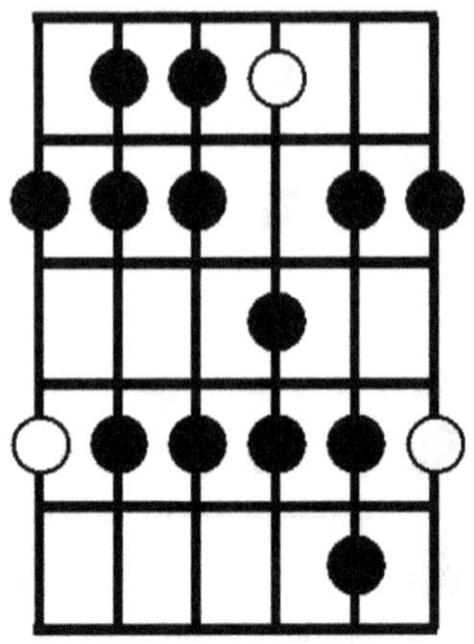

Locrian Modal Scale

The Locrian mode is the seventh mode of a major scale. It can be used to improvise over minor seven flat five chords.

Scale spelling: 1, ♭2, ♭3, 4, ♭5, ♭6, ♭7

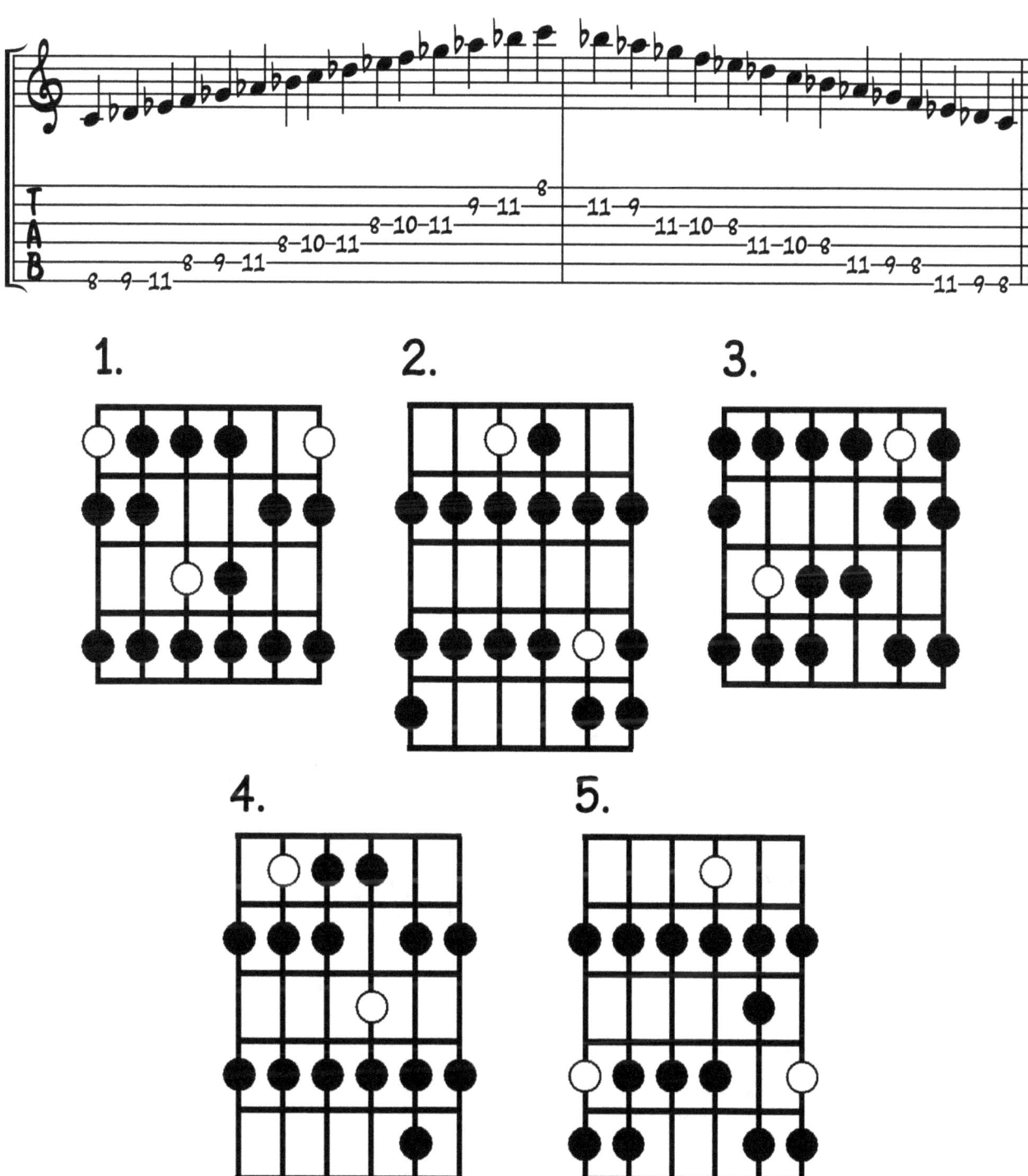

Harmonic Minor Scale

The harmonic minor scale has a more 'classical' sound than other minor scales, and can be used to add interest to lead lines.

Scale spelling: 1, 2, ♭3, 4, 5, ♭6, 7

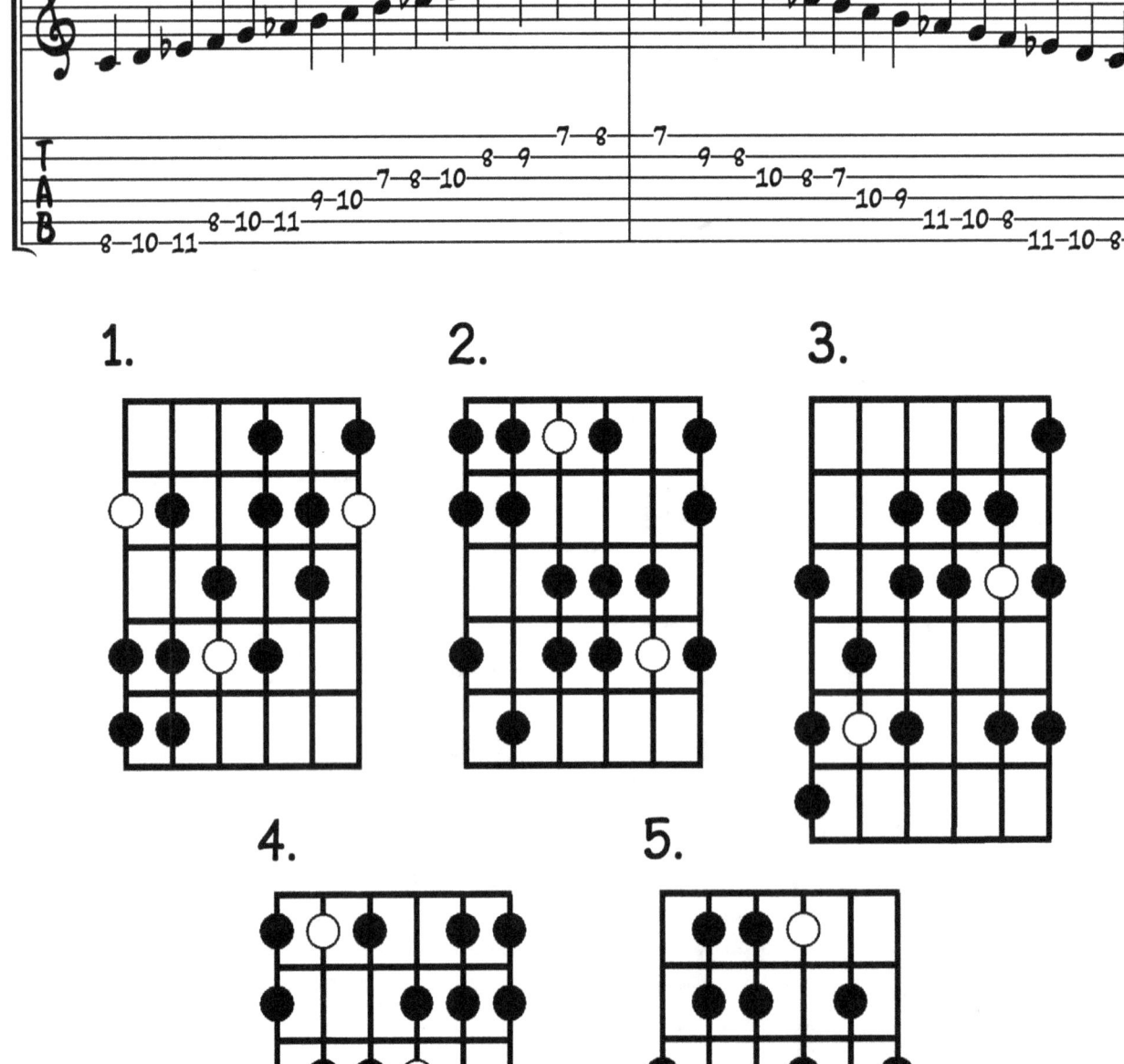

Jazz Minor Scale / Melodic Minor Scale

The jazz minor scale is also known as the melodic minor scale, although strictly speaking it is only the same as the descending form of the melodic minor used in traditional 'classical' music theory. The jazz minor is a good scale to use when improvising over minor sixth chords. If the seventh note of a jazz minor scale is used as the tonic note, it becomes an altered scale. Compare the two scales to see the relationship.

Scale spelling: 1, 2, ♭3, 4, 5, 6, 7

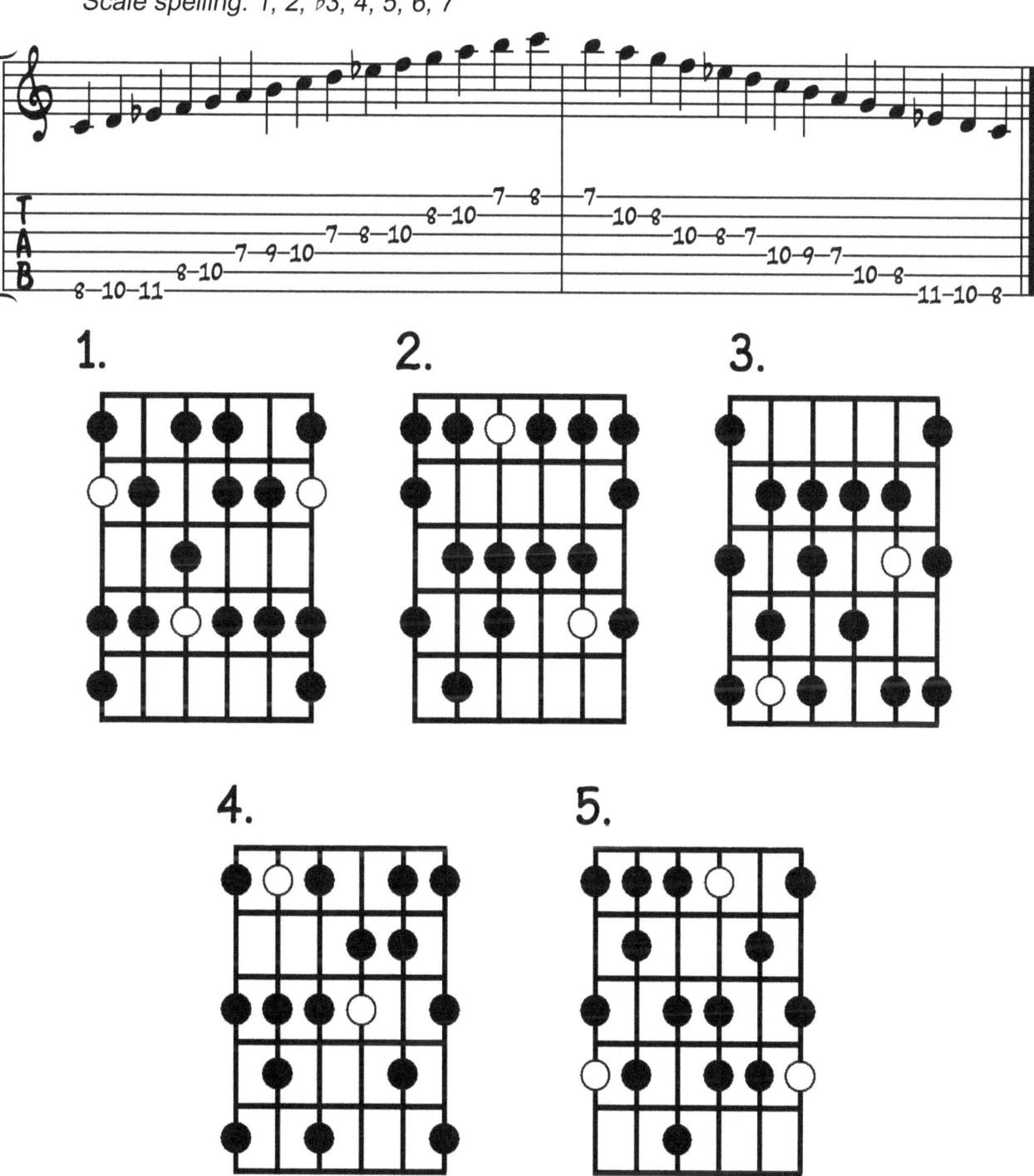

Phrygian Dominant Scale

The Phrygian dominant scale is also known as the 'Spanish Gypsy' or 'Freygish' scale (note that the double harmonic scale is sometimes called the Spanish gypsy scale too). The Phrygian dominant scale can also be thought of as being the fifth mode of a harmonic minor scale – the scale shapes are the same but the tonic notes are different depending on which scale is being played. The Phrygian dominant scale produces an Eastern sound that can add interest to your improvisation.

Scale spelling: 1, ♭2, 3, 4, 5, ♭6, ♭7

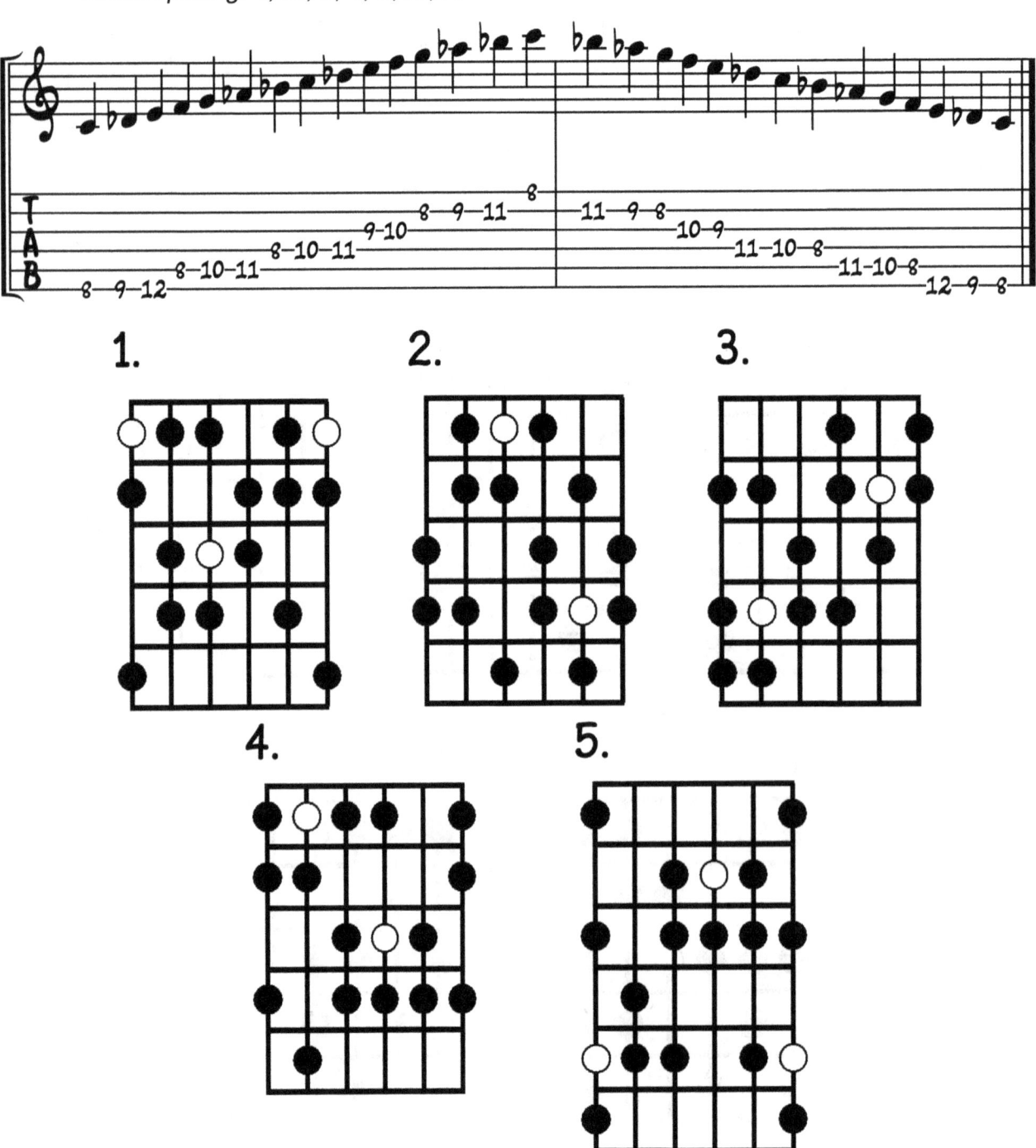

Double Harmonic Scale

The double harmonic scale is another Eastern-sounding scale. It goes by several other names, including the Arabic Scale, (Spanish) Gypsy Scale and Byzantine Scale.

Scale spelling: 1, ♭2, 3, 4, 5, ♭6, 7

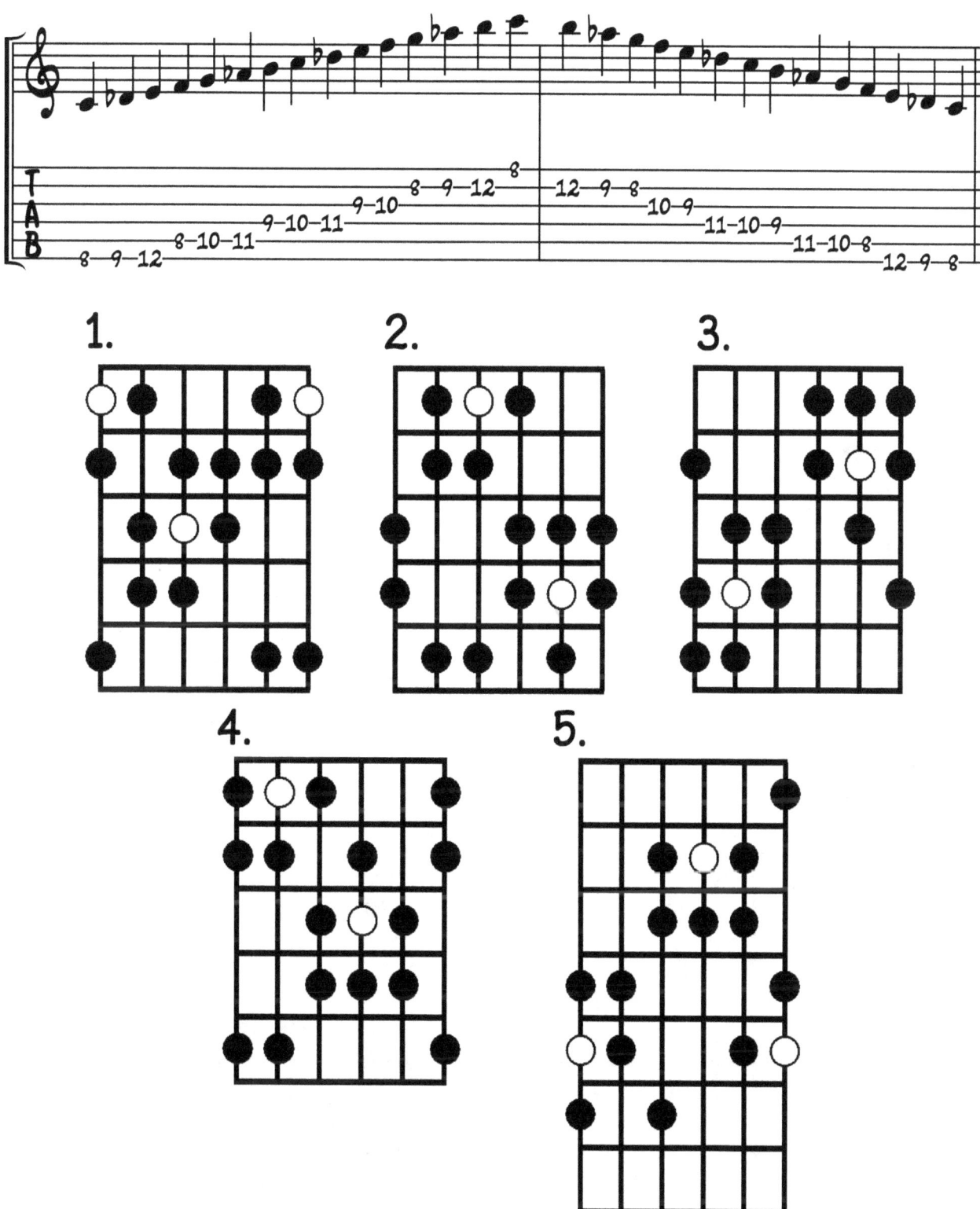

Persian Scale

The Persian scale can add an exotic color to your improvisations. It is very similar to the double harmonic and Phrygian dominant scales.

Persian Scale Spelling: 1, b2, 3, 4, b5, b6, 7

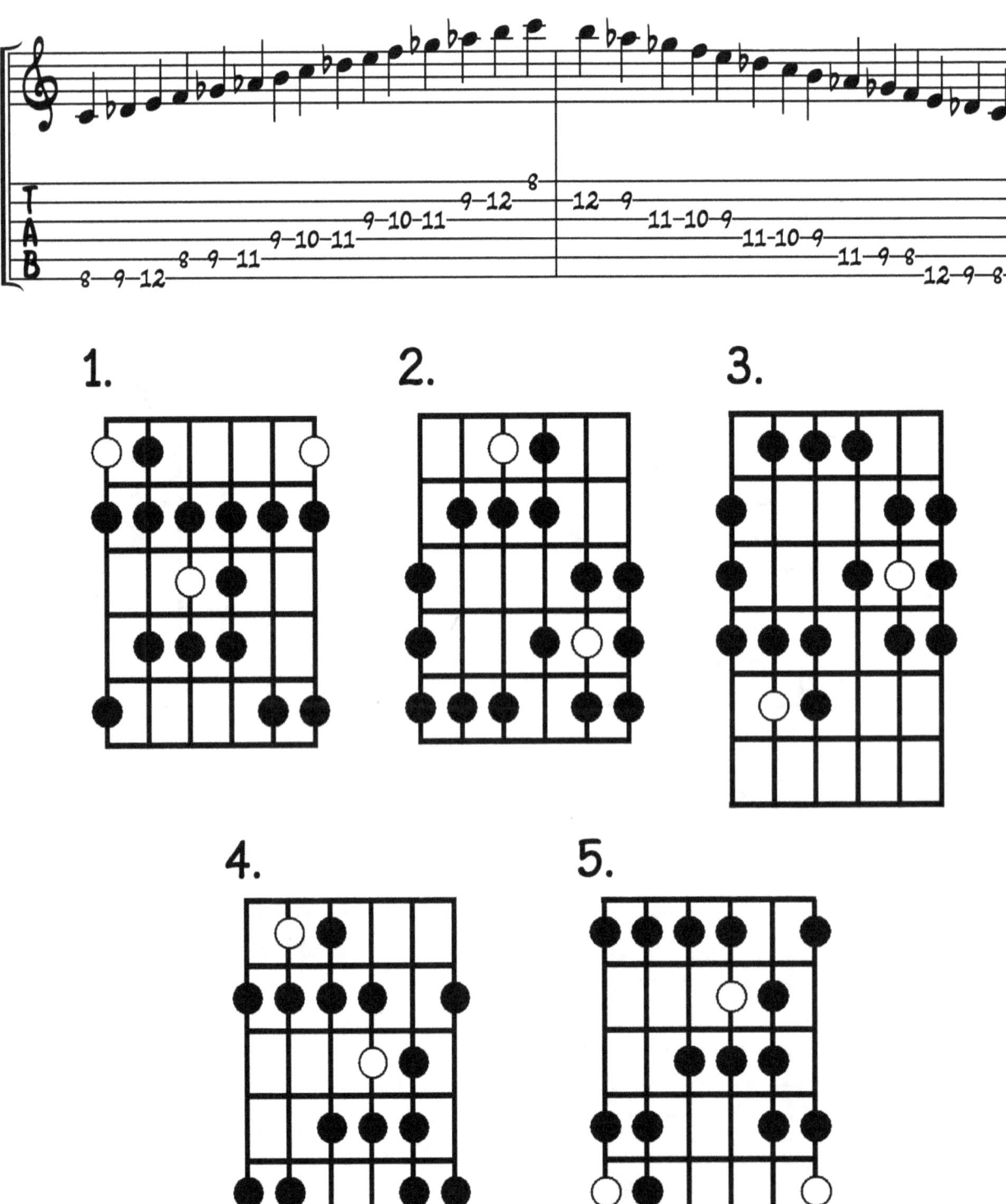

Neapolitan Minor Scale

The Neapolitan minor scale is another exotic scale that could be used to spice up a solo, or perhaps to provide inspiration for composition.

Scale spelling: 1, ♭2, ♭3, 4, 5, ♭6, 7

1.

2.

3.

4.

5.

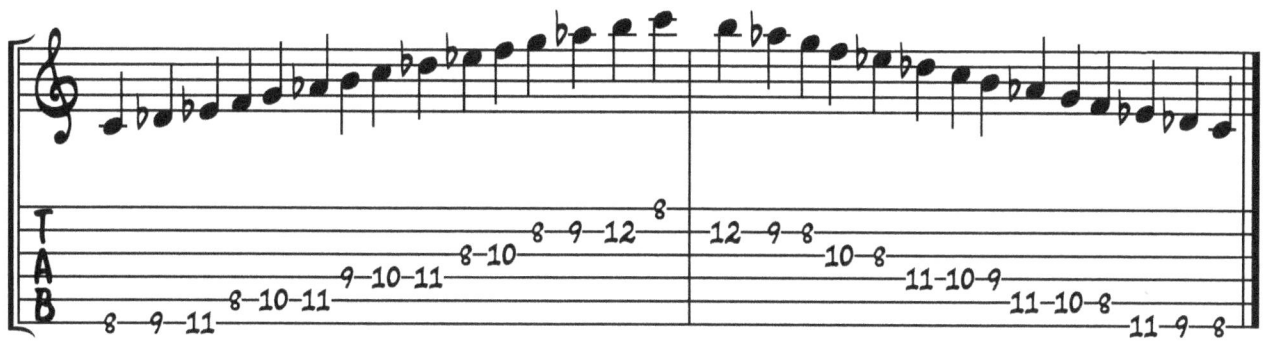

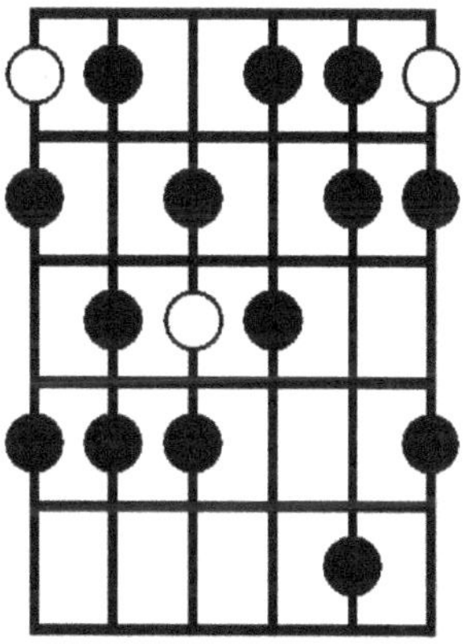

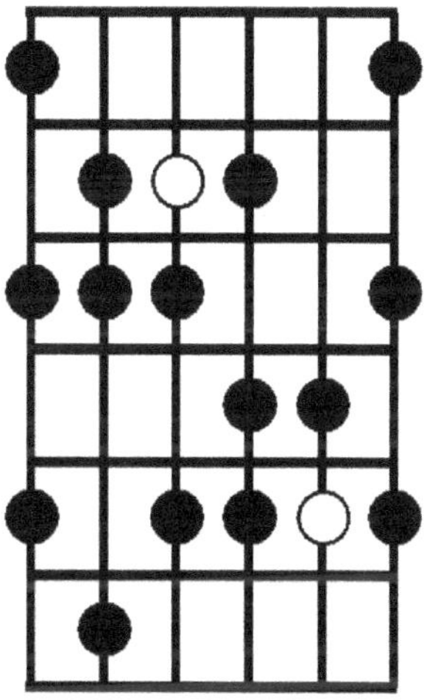

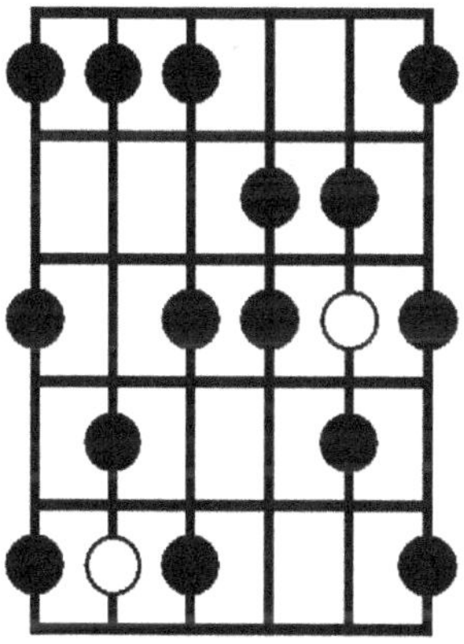

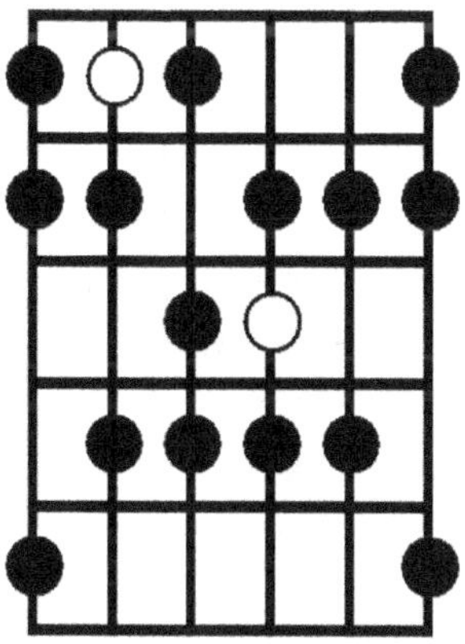

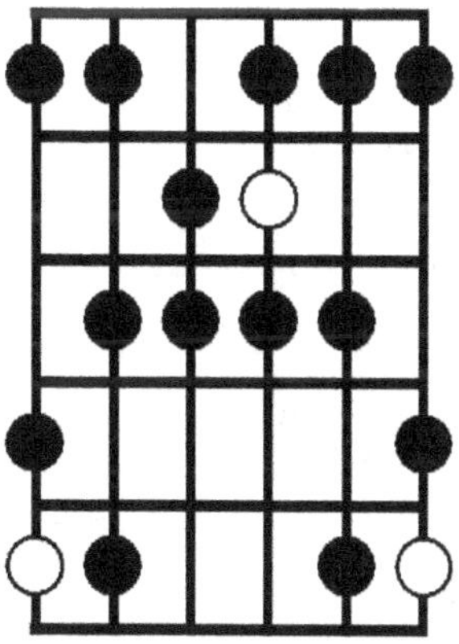

Neapolitan Major Scale

The Neapolitan Major scale, despite its name, actually has a minor tonality. It differs from the Neapolitan minor scale only by having a non-flattened sixth note.

Scale spelling: 1, ♭2, ♭3, 4, 5, 6, 7

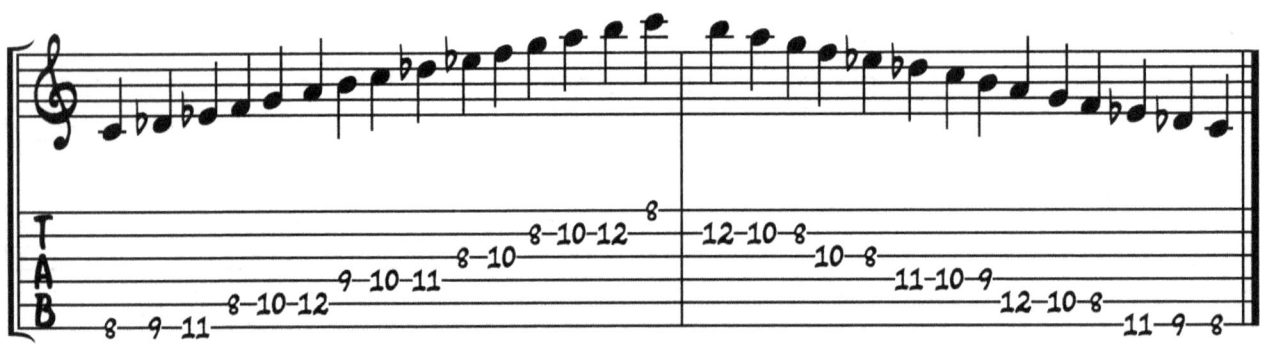

1.

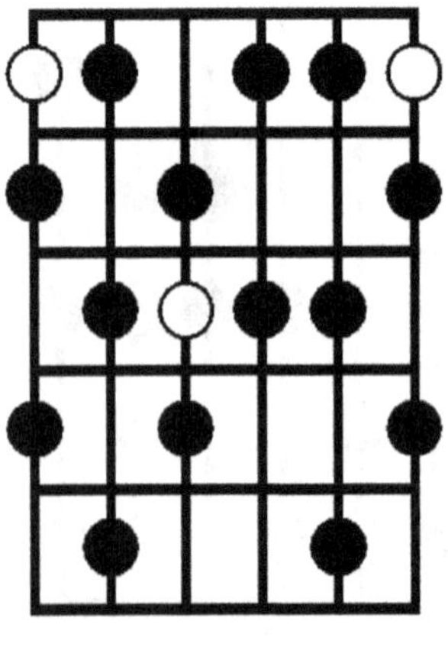

2.

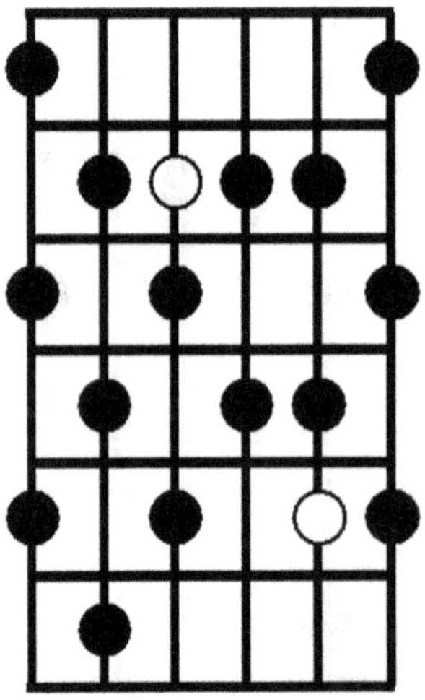

3.

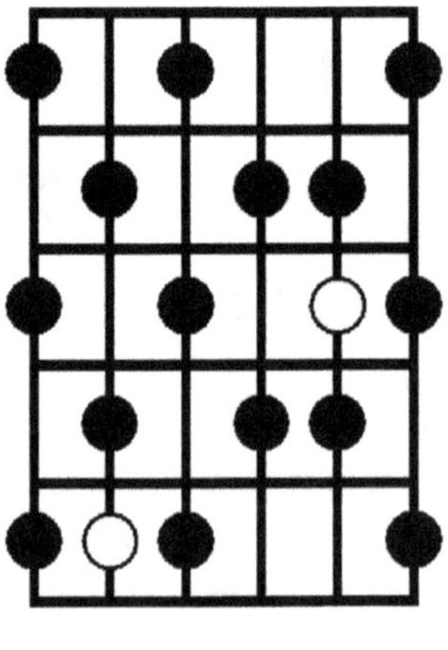

4.

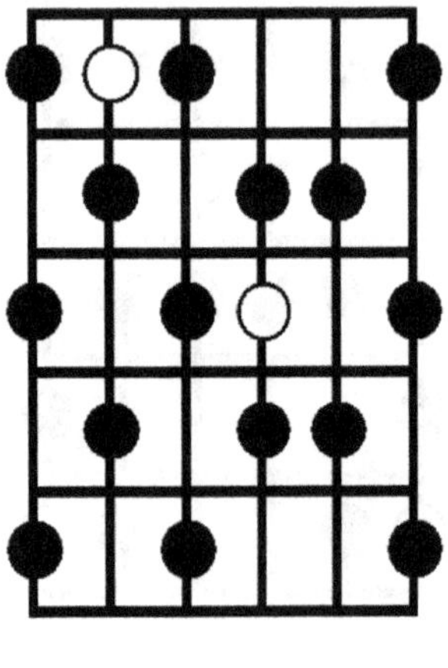

5.

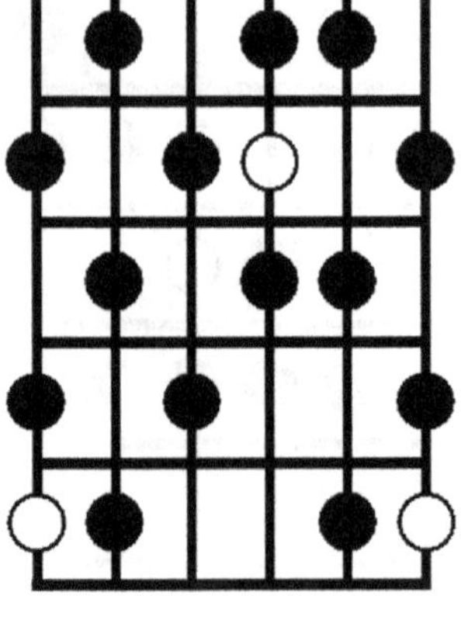

Bebop Dominant Scale

The bebop dominant scale is similar to a Mixolydian modal scale, but has an additional note: the major seventh. Bebop scales have an extra note to enable jazz musicians to create smooth lines in which chord tones always fall on the beat.

Scale spelling: 1, 2, 3, 4, 5, 6, b7, 7

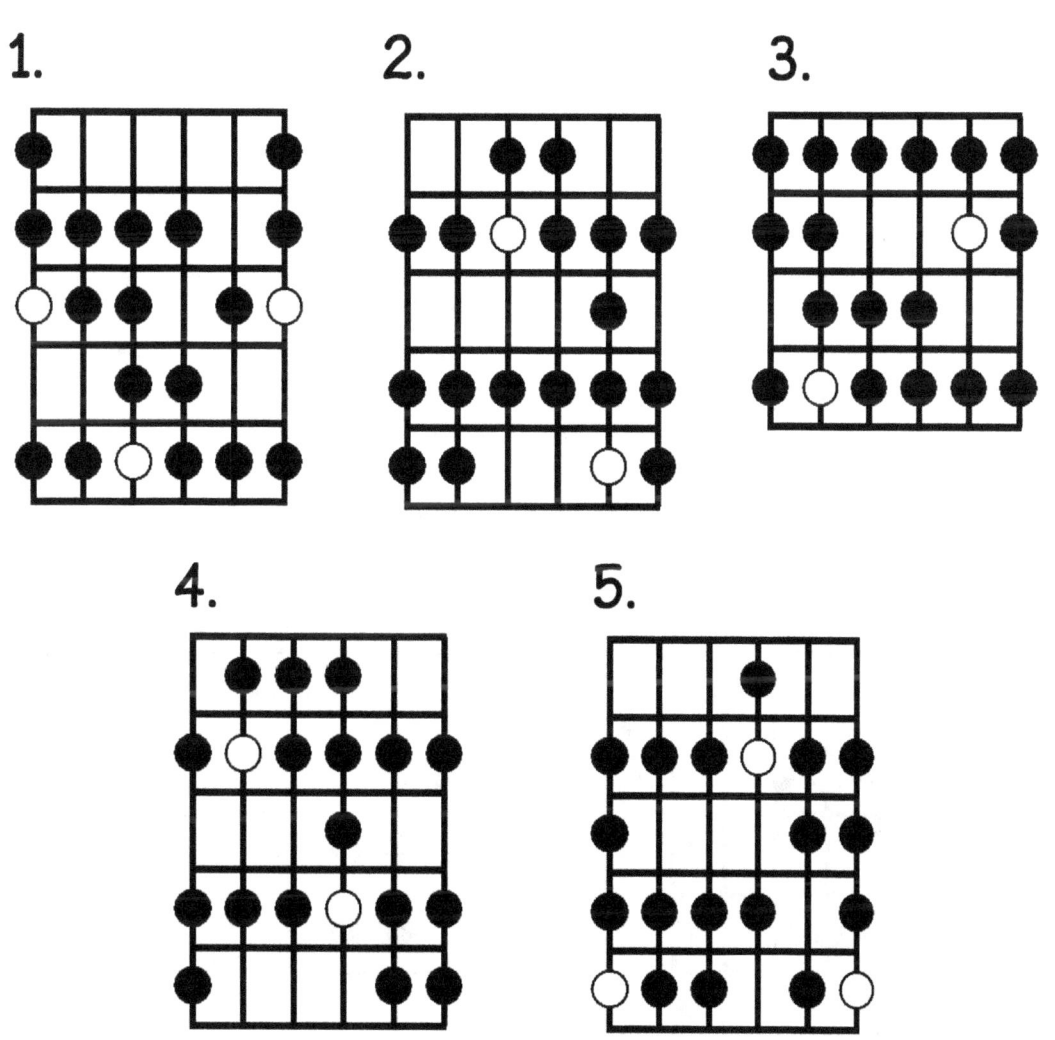

Bebop Minor Scale

The bebop minor scale is related to the Dorian modal scale, but like the bebop dominant scale has an extra note to allow flowing jazz lines. The scale shapes are the same as those for the bebop dominant (both scales use the same notes if a bebop minor scale is played over a II chord and a bebop dominant over a V7 chord).

Scale spelling: 1, 2, ♭3, 3, 4, 5, 6, ♭7

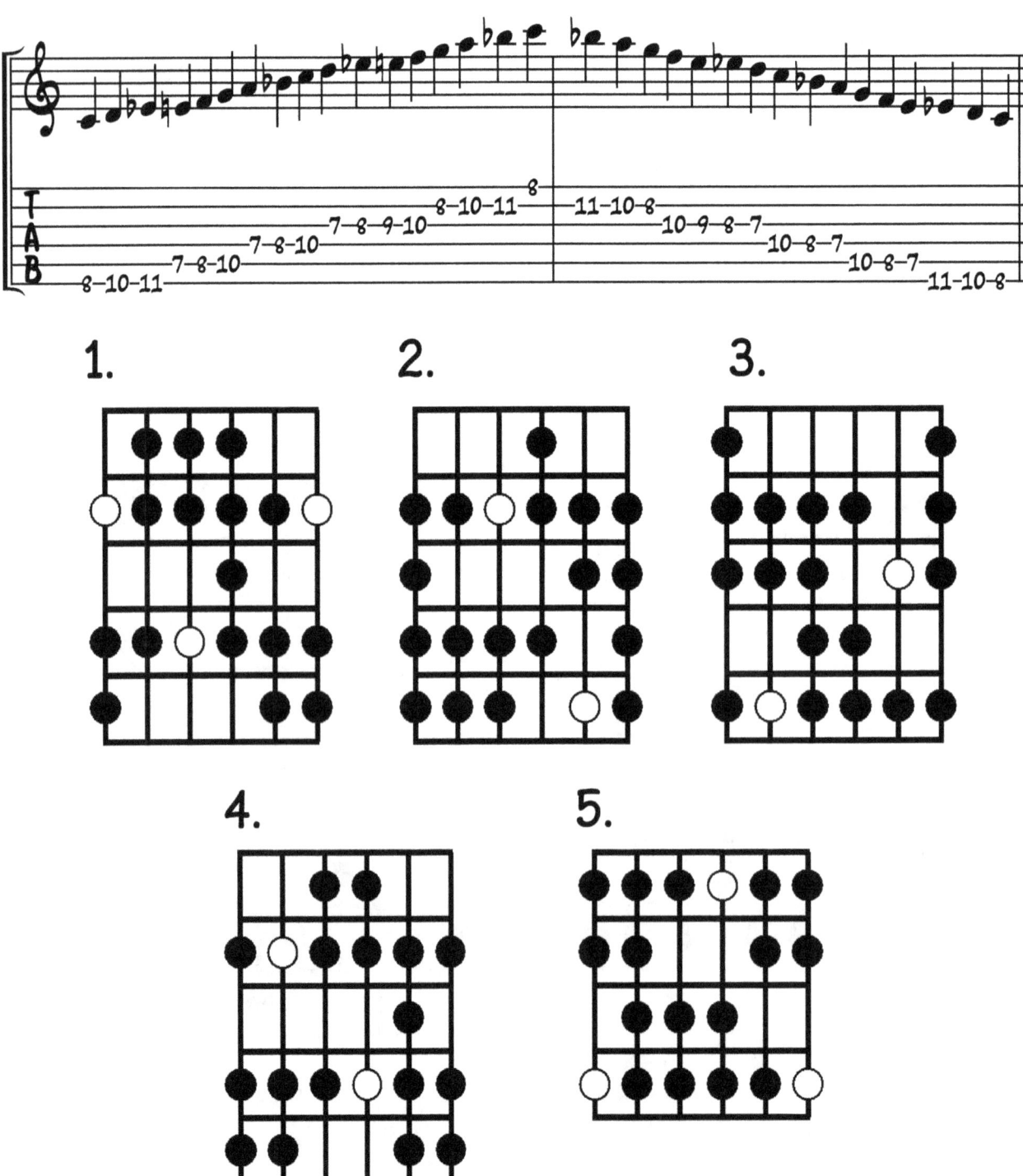

Bebop Major Scale

The bebop major scale is the same as a standard major scale, but with an extra note: the augmented fifth. As with the other bebop scales, the additional note allows jazz improvisors to create fluid lines. Try playing the scale with a swing feel over a major chord with the same root to get a feel for the jazz sound.

Scale spelling: 1, 2, 3, 4, 5, #5, 6, 7

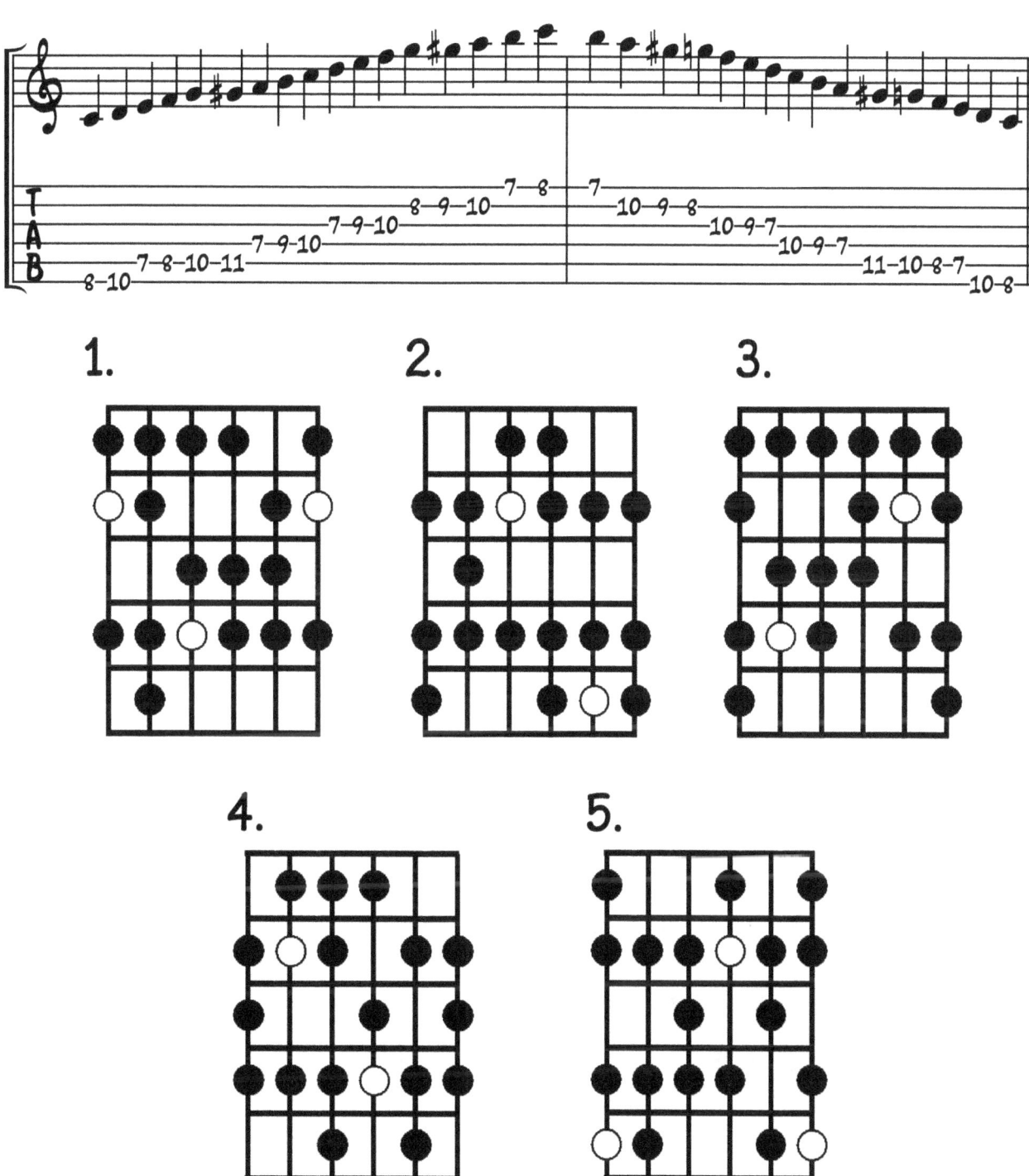

Altered Scale

The altered scale is the same as a jazz minor scale that starts from the seventh degree. It is mainly used to improvise over dominant chords*. The altered scale is so-called because it contains every possible altered note (sharpened and flattened 5ths, 9ths and 11ths). These altered notes are used by improvisors to create jazzy-sounding tensions in their lines.

Scale spelling: 1, ♭2, ♭3, ♭4, ♭5, ♭6, ♭7

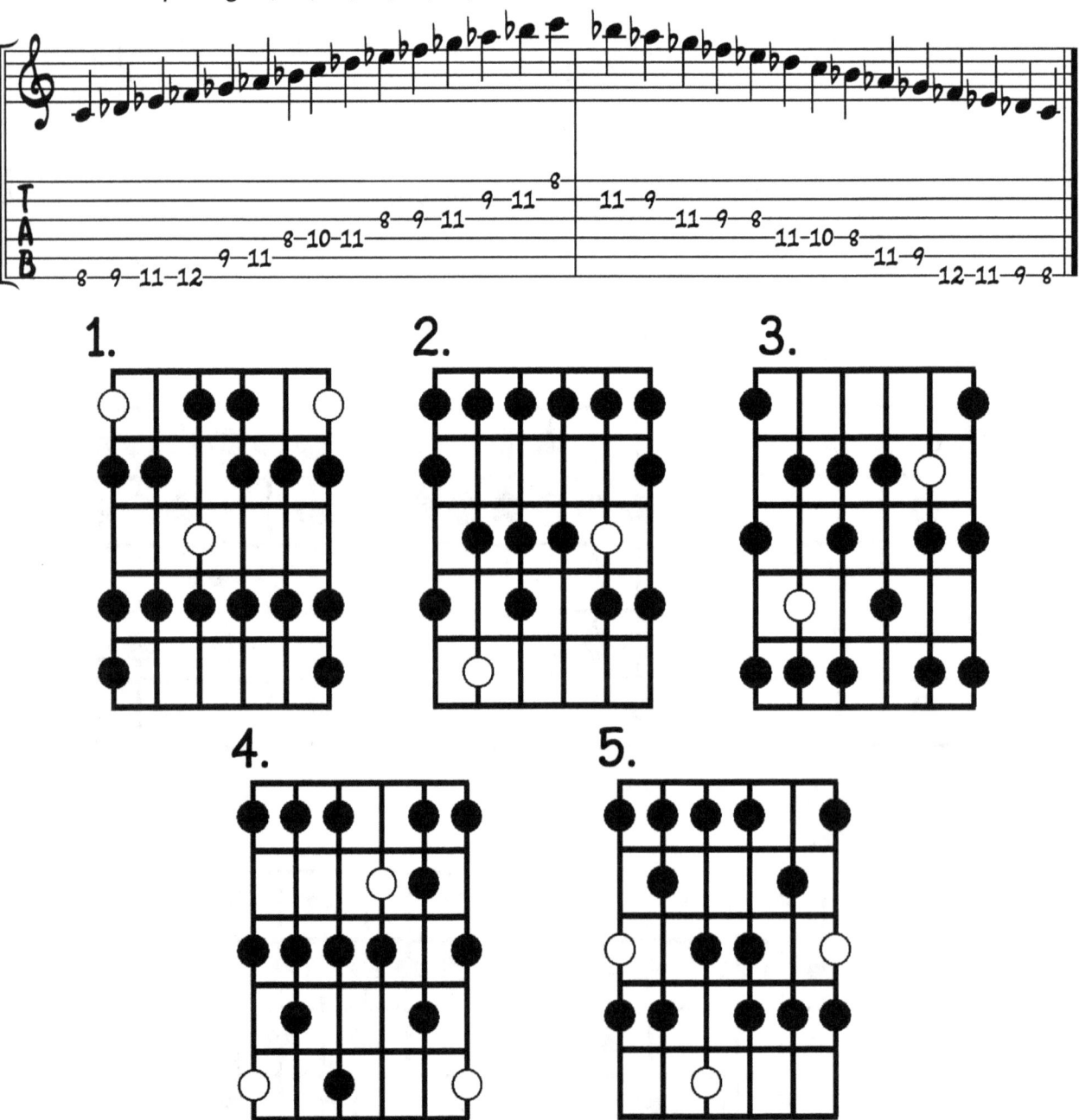

* *Most guitarists simply play a jazz minor scale a semitone higher than the dominant chord – it can then be considered to be an altered scale and only one scale needs to be learned.*

Lydian Augmented Scale

The Lydian augmented scale is a variation of the Lydian modal scale. It has an augmented fifth and can be used over major chords with raised fifths. It can also be used to solo over dominant seventh flat-five chords by using the Lydian augmented scale whose tonic is the seventh of the chord, or over altered dominant chords by using the scale whose tonic is the third of the chord (in this case it is the same as an altered scale).

Scale spelling: 1, 2, 3, #4, #5, 6, 7

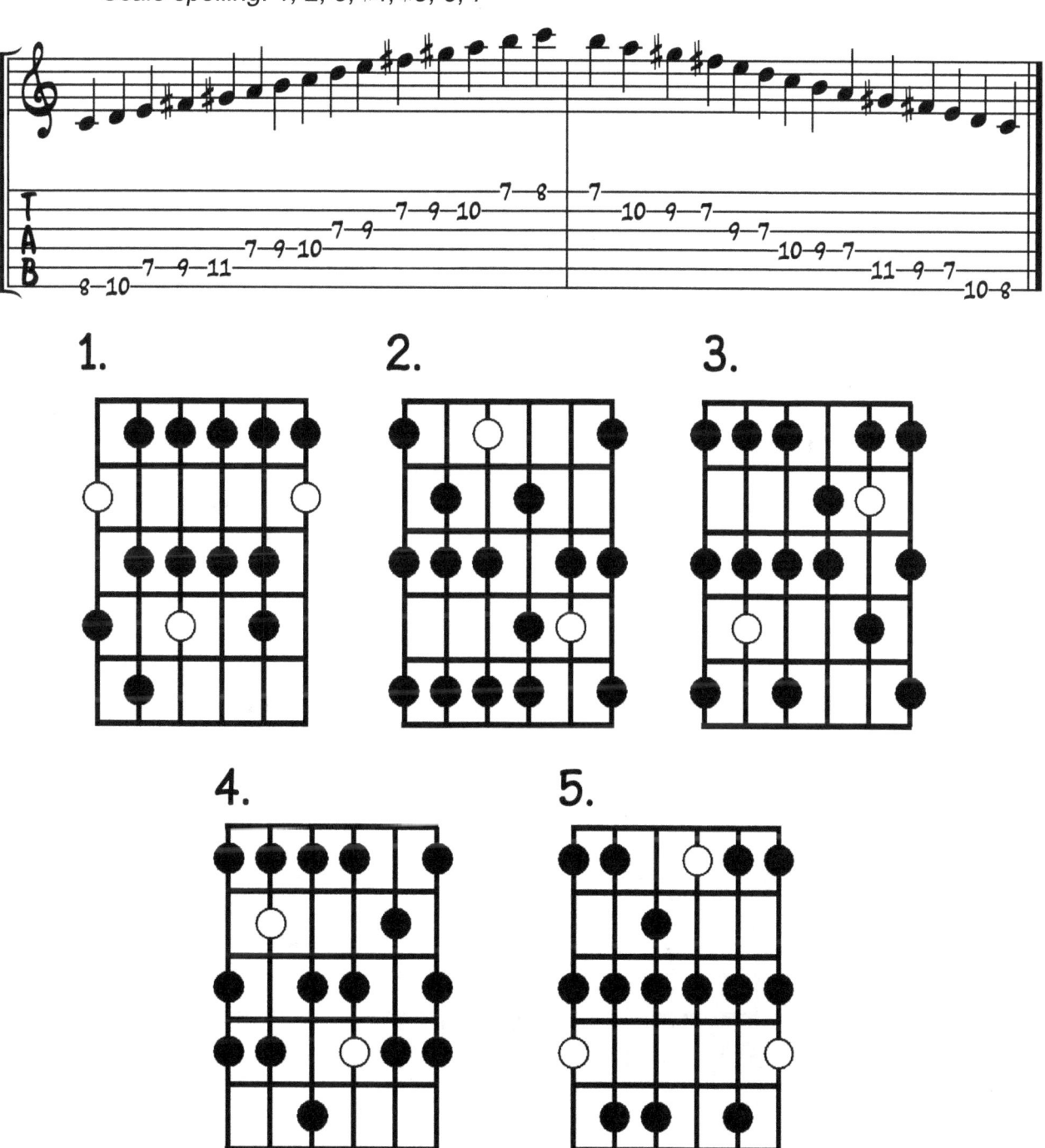

Mixolydian #4 / Lydian ♭7 Scale

A jazzy scale that has two names; it can either be thought of as a Mixolydian scale with a sharpened fourth, or as a Lydian scale with a flattened seventh note. This scale can be used over dominant chords with the same root as the tonic of the scale, and works particularly well over seven flat-five or seven sharp-eleven chords.

Scale spelling: 1, 2, 3, #4, 5, 6, ♭7

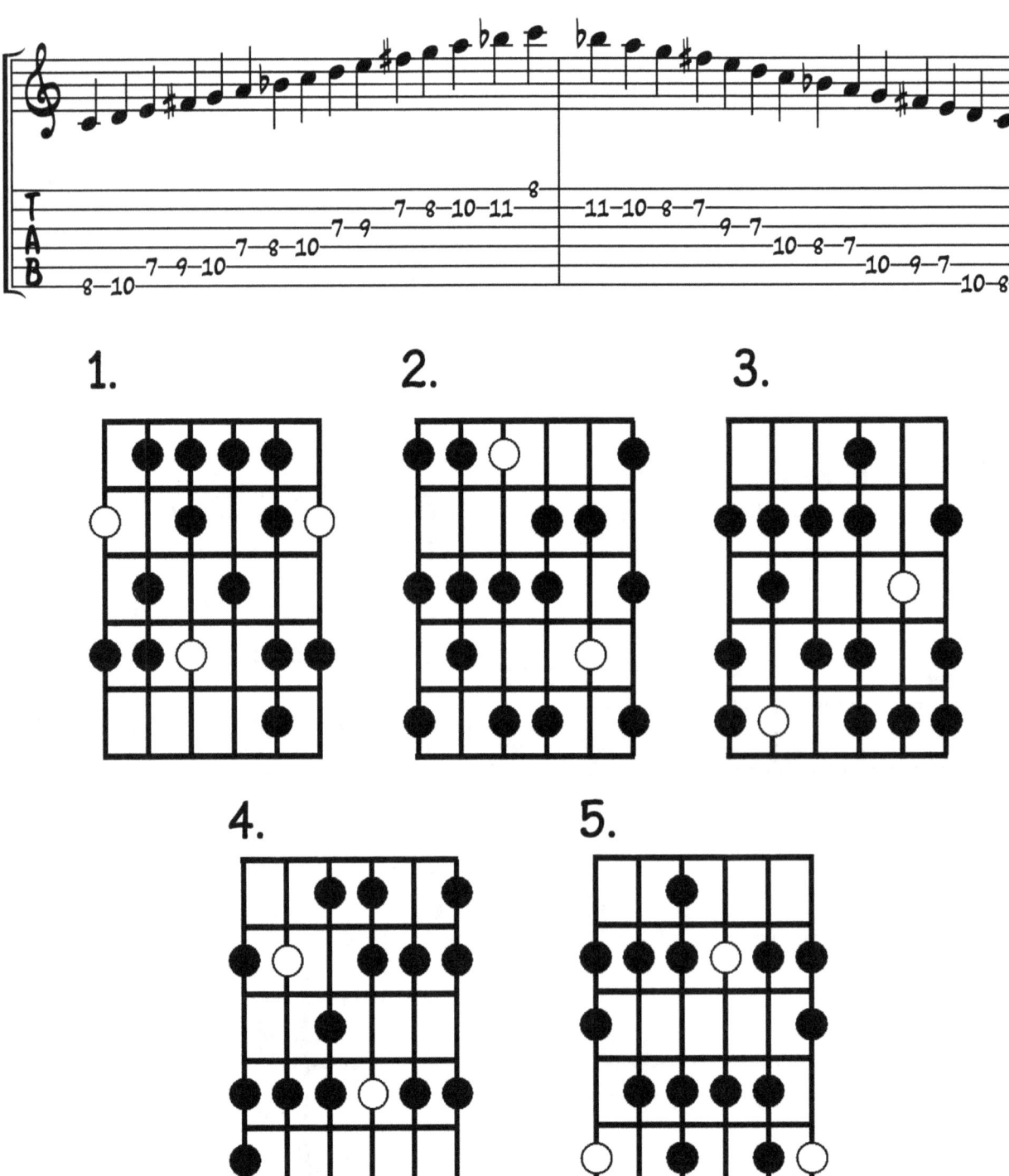

Locrian #2 Scale

This scale is a variation of the Locrian modal scale, and like that scale, can be used to improvise over minor seven flat-five chords whose root is the same as the tonic of the scale.

Scale spelling: 1, 2, ♭3, 4, ♭5, ♭6, ♭7

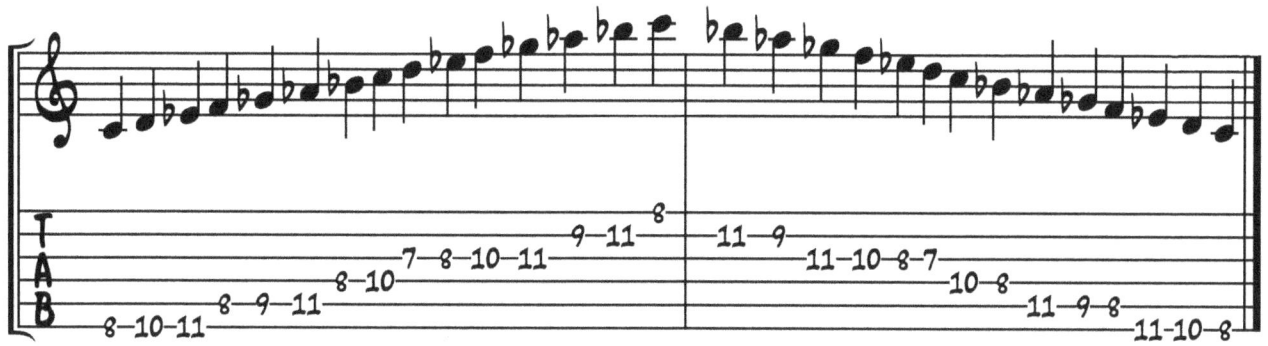

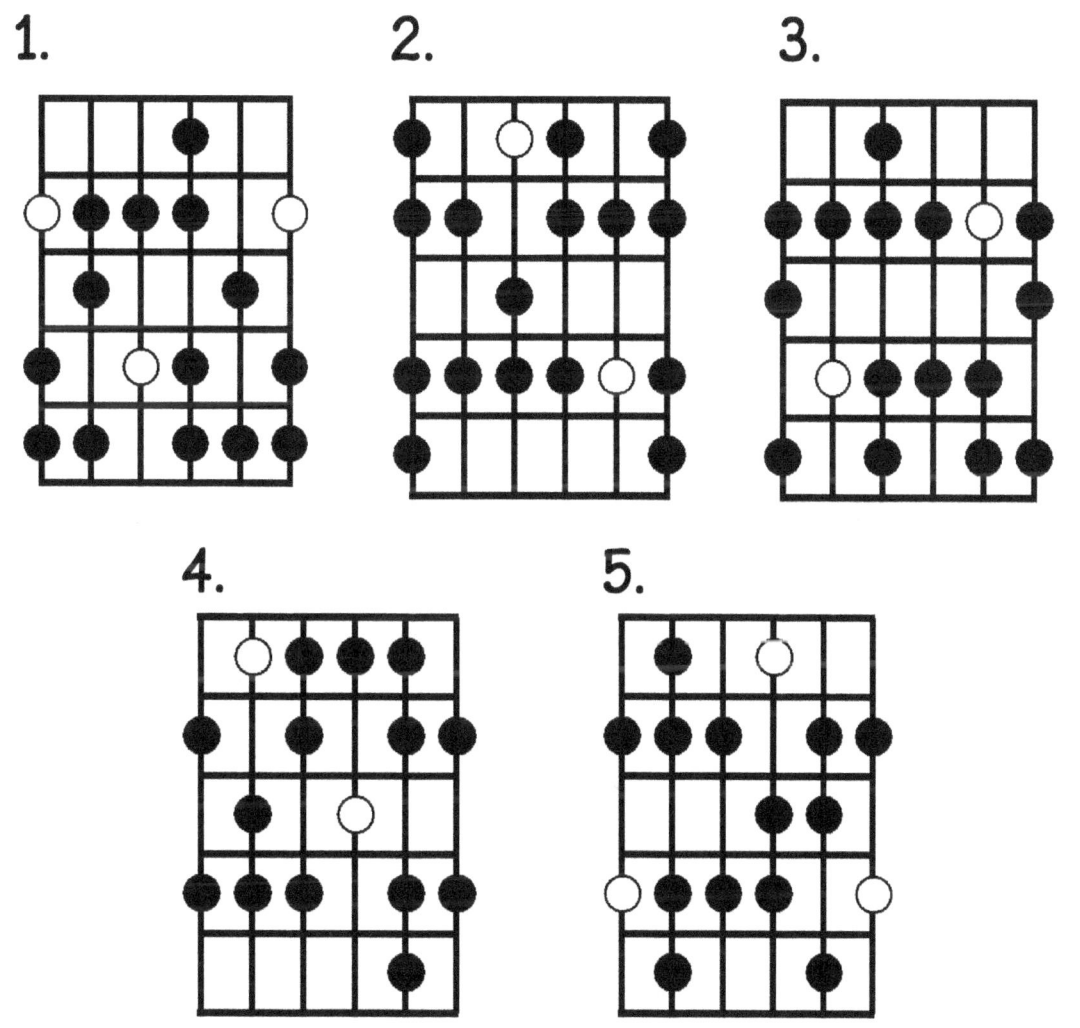

Diminished Scale

Diminished scales move in alternate whole and half-steps. They can be used to improvise over diminished chords with the same root as the tonic of the scale. They are also used over dominant chords: use the diminished scale a half-step higher than the root of the chord. Used in the second way, diminished scales create tensions that can give the line a jazz sound.

Scale spelling: 1, 2, ♭3, 4, ♭5, ♭6, 6, 7

1.   **2.**

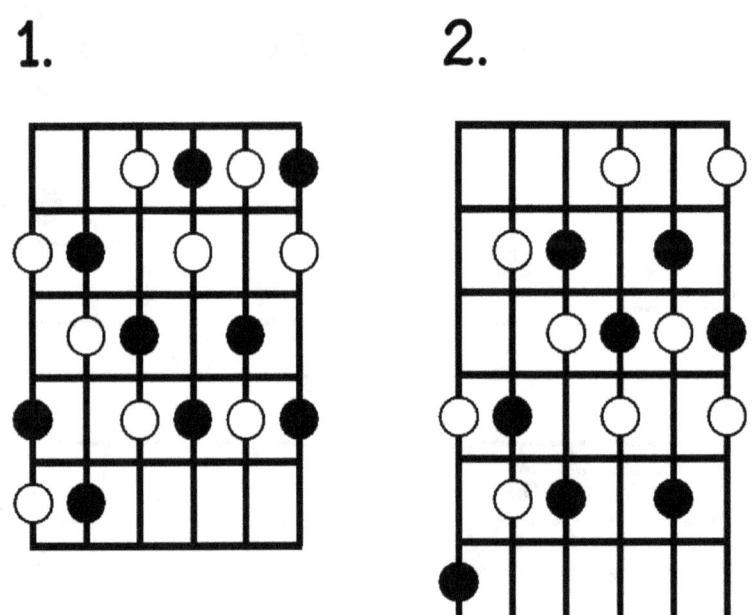

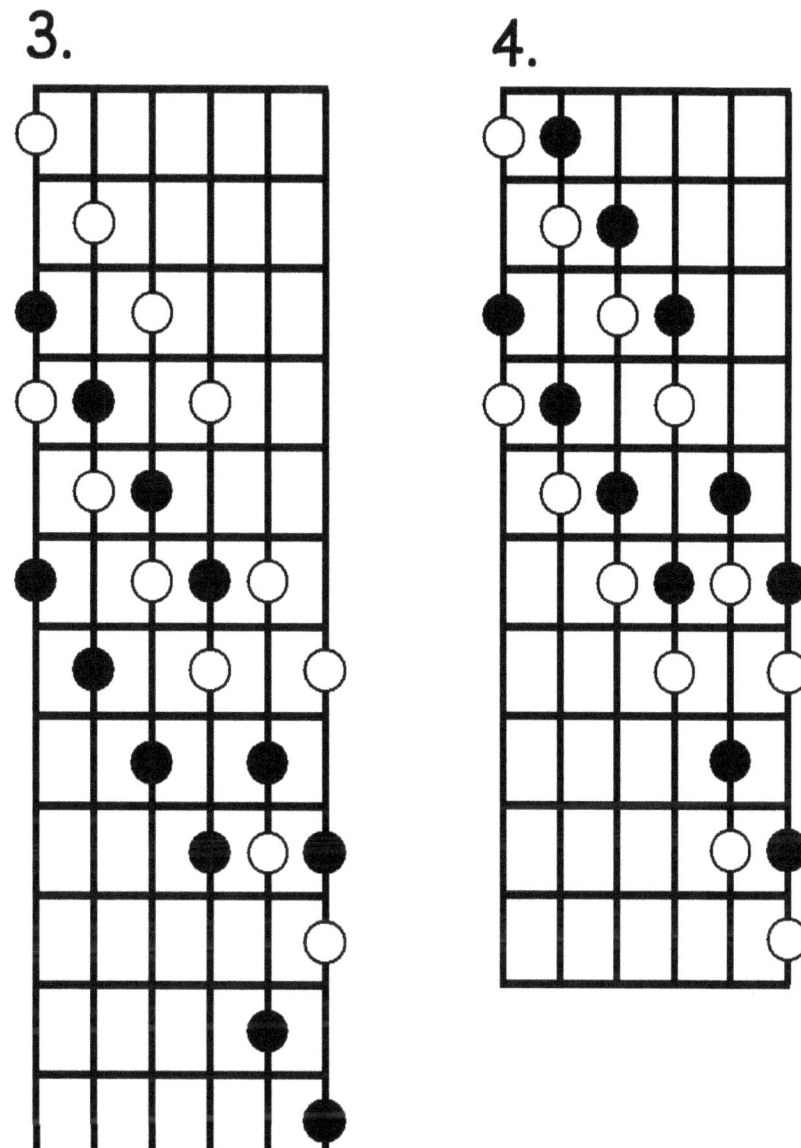

Every other note of a diminished scale can be considered to be a root note: for example, an A diminished scale contains the same notes as a C diminished scale. For this reason each scale shape has more than one root note marked.

Whole Tone Scale

The notes in a whole tone scale are all a whole tone apart. Because of this, every note in the scale shapes below can potentially be a tonic note (there are actually only two whole tone scales). Whole tone scales have a very characteristic sound, and can be used to play over dominant flat-five or sharp-five chords.

Scale spelling: 1, 2, 3, ♯4, ♯5, ♭7

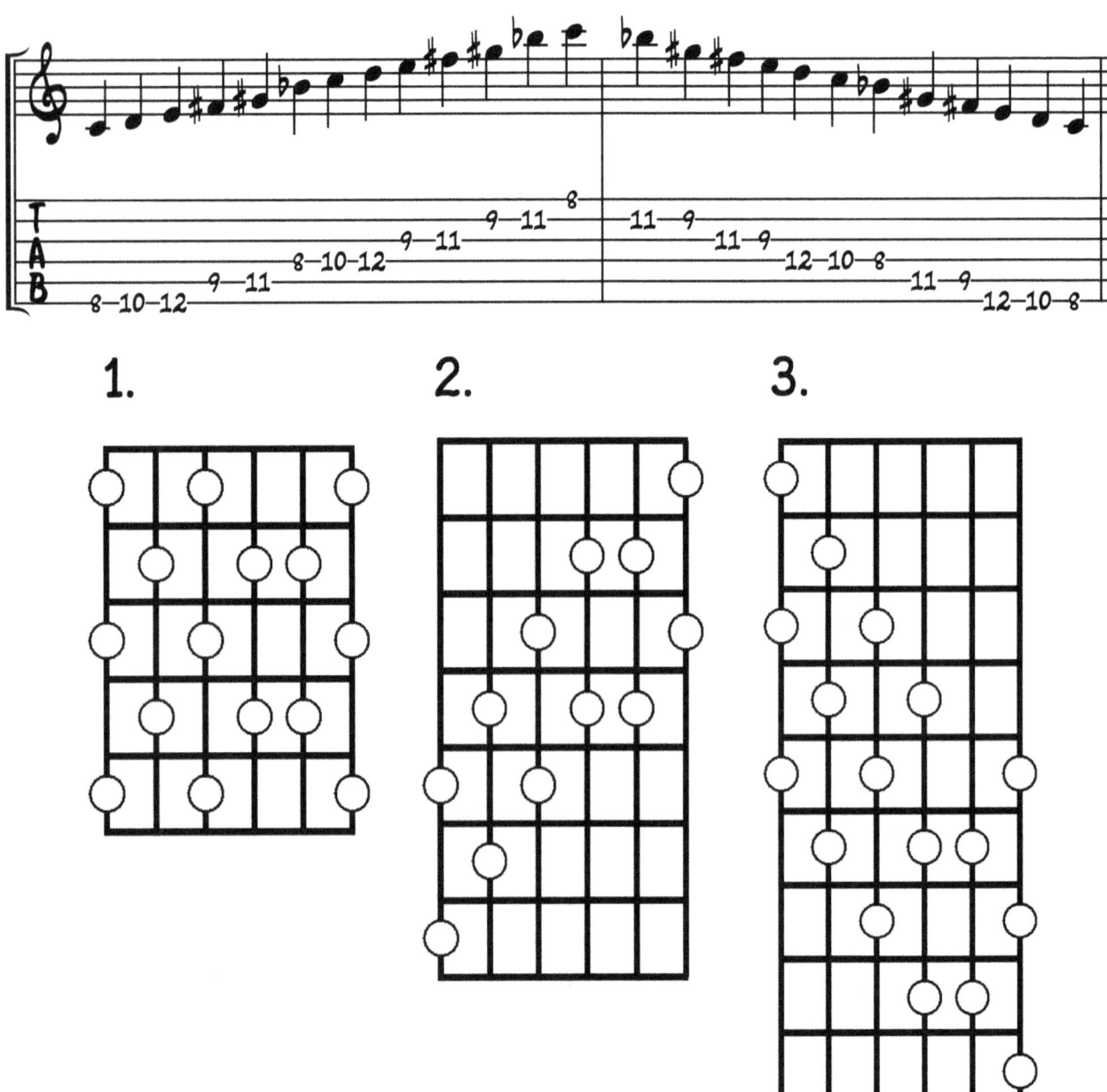

Chromatic Scale

The chromatic scale moves in half-steps. Every note in chromatic scale shapes can be a tonic note. Playing chromatic scales is a good warm-up exercise.

Play this scale either by using your index finger to play the first two notes on each string apart from the second (B) string, OR by using your little finger to play the last two notes on each string apart from the second (B) string.

1.

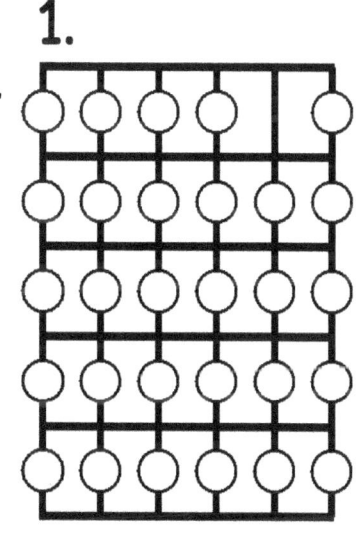

2.

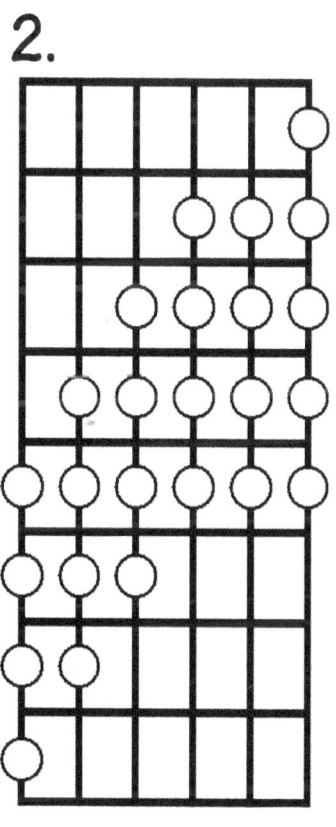

Japanese Scales

The following Japanese scales are all pentatonic (i.e. they are comprised of five notes). These scales are used in Japanese folk melodies and can be very inspiring to experiment with: use them to create atmospheric melodies or improvisations.

In Scale

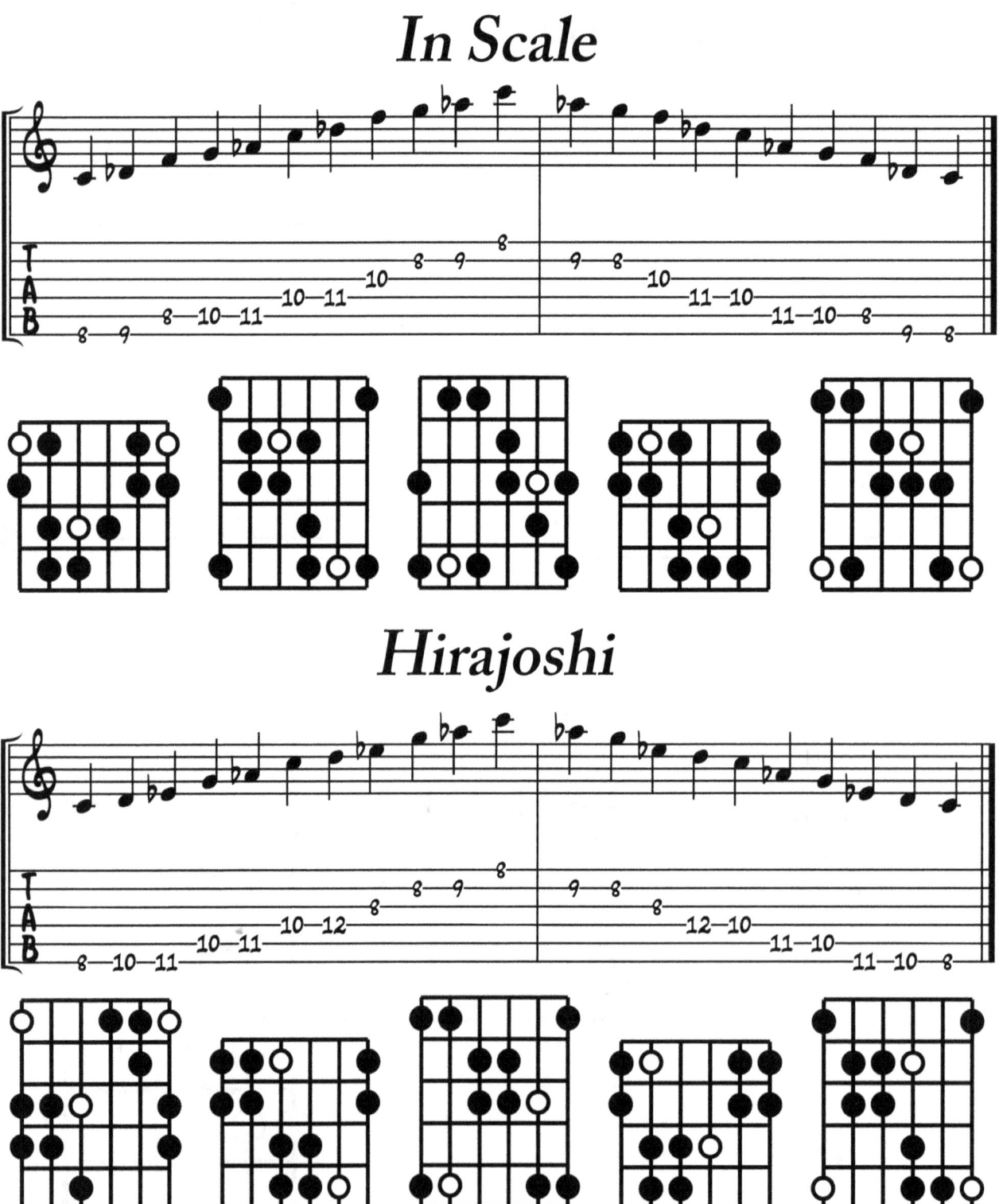

Hirajoshi

Yo Scale

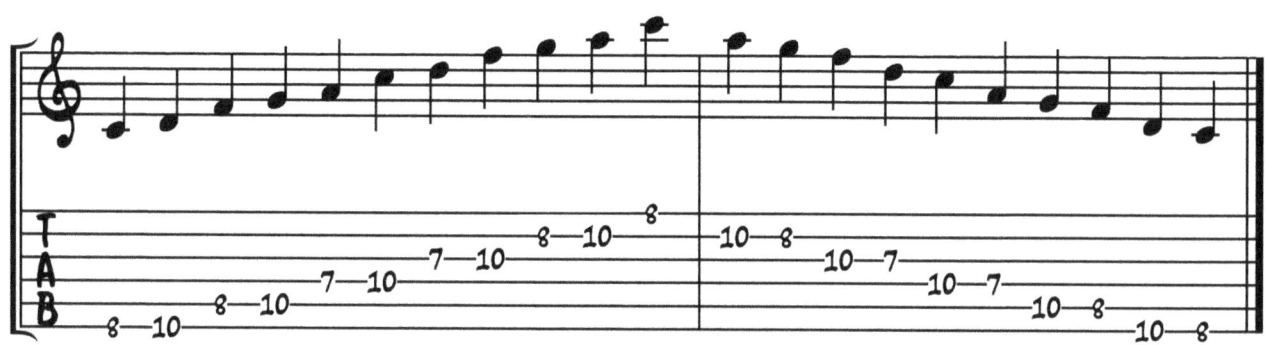

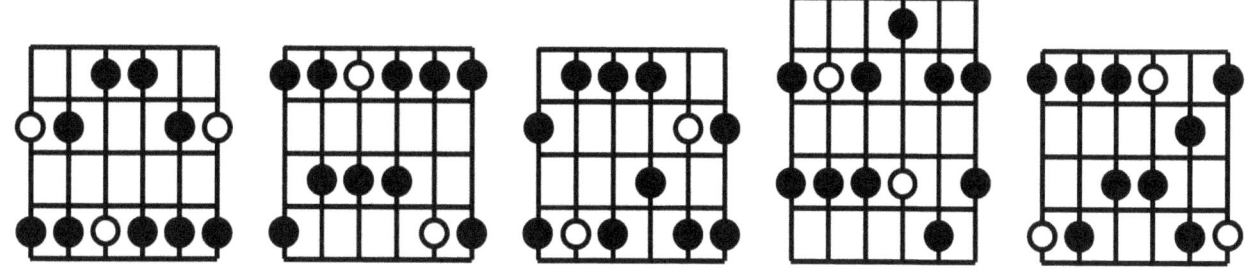

Scale Spellings For Japanese Pentatonic Scales:

In Scale: 1, ♭2, 4, 5, ♭6

Hirajoshi: 1, 2, ♭3, 5, ♭6

Yo Scale: 1, 2, 4, 5, 6

Arpeggios

Arpeggios are chords in which the notes are played one at a time, rather than all at once. All of the arpeggio diagrams in this section are 'movable' shapes, with the root notes being represented by the white circles.

Arpeggios can be used in improvisation and to create riffs and melodies.

Arpeggios Section 1

In this section 2-octave arpeggios are shown in tab and notation with a root of C. The diagrams show the arpeggios continuing upwards and downwards to include all of the potential notes for each position.

Arpeggios Section 2

The second section contains extended dominant and minor arpeggios. In this section the notation and diagrams show the full arpeggio, and are not extended below the root note or further extended above the highest note.

Arpeggios Section 1
Major

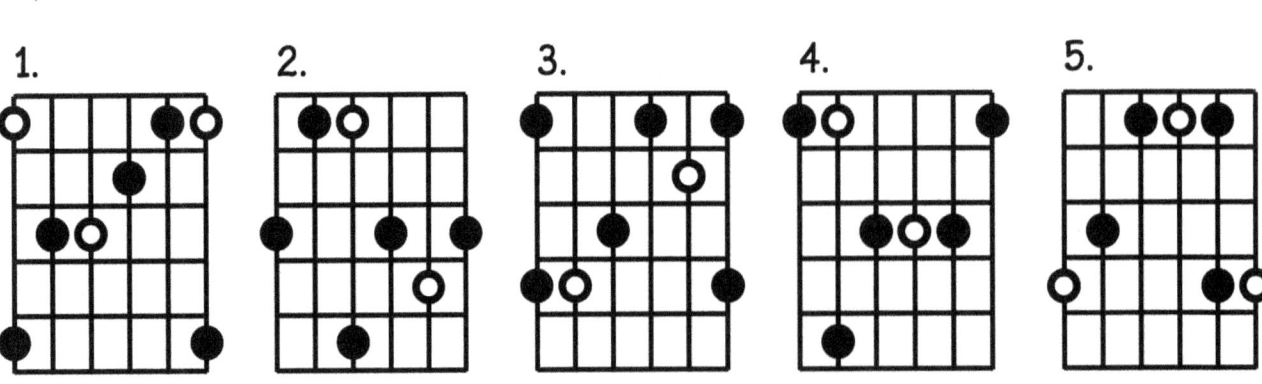

Minor

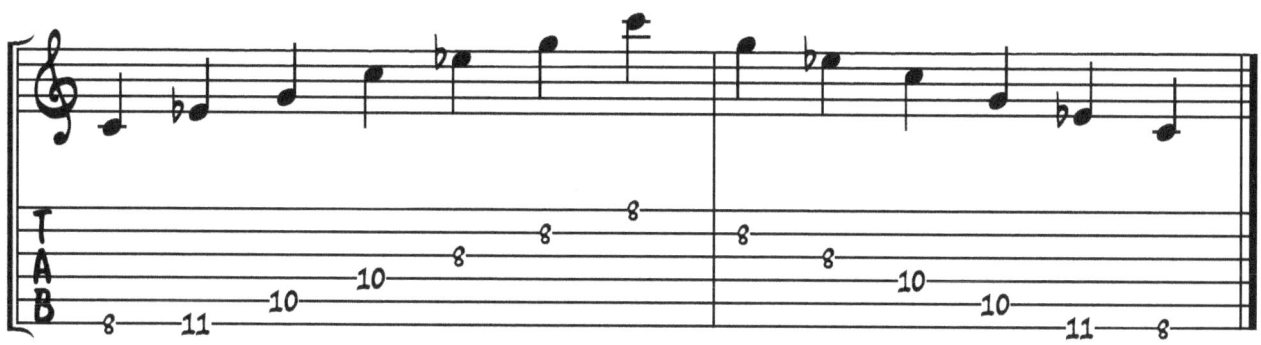

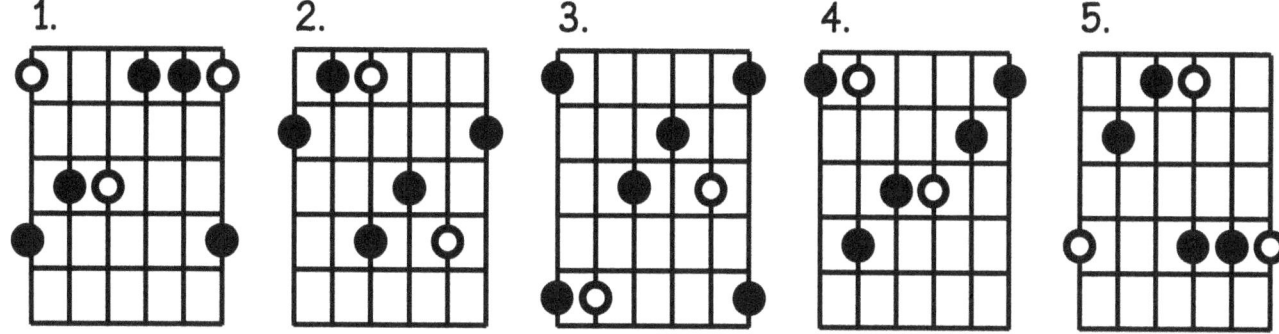

Dominant 7th

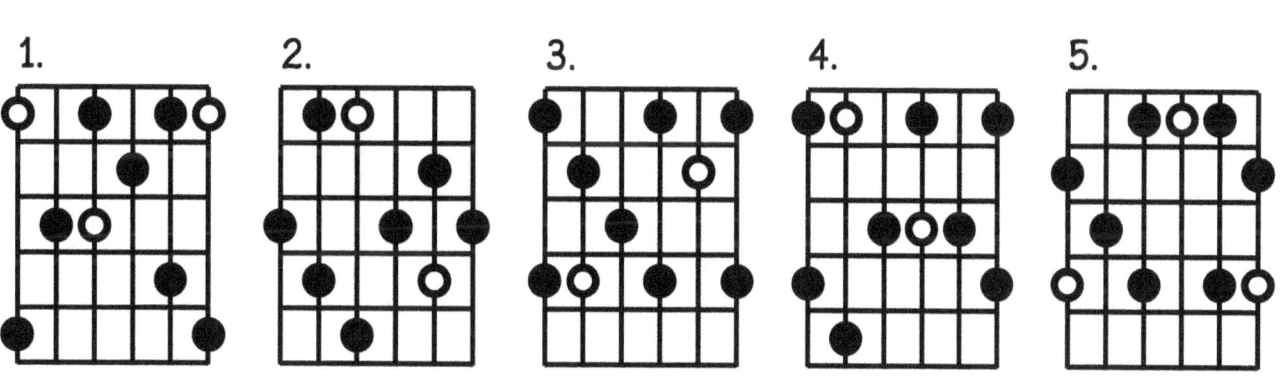

Minor 7th

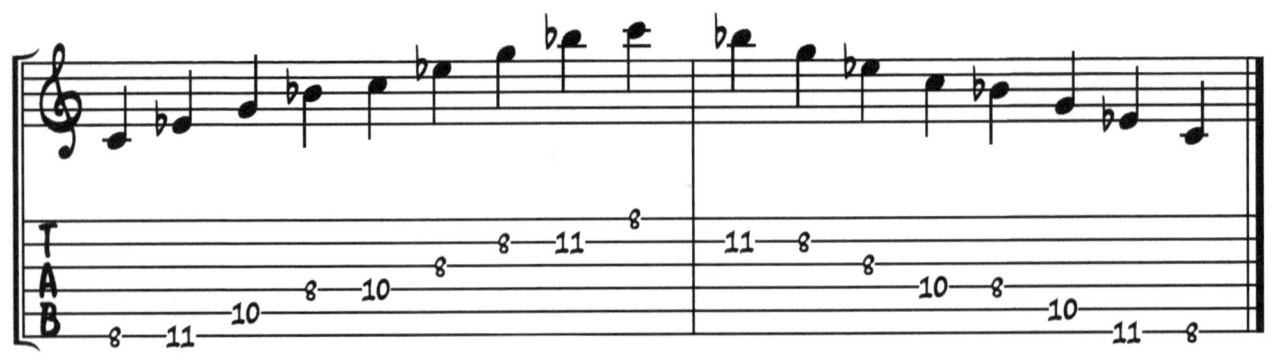
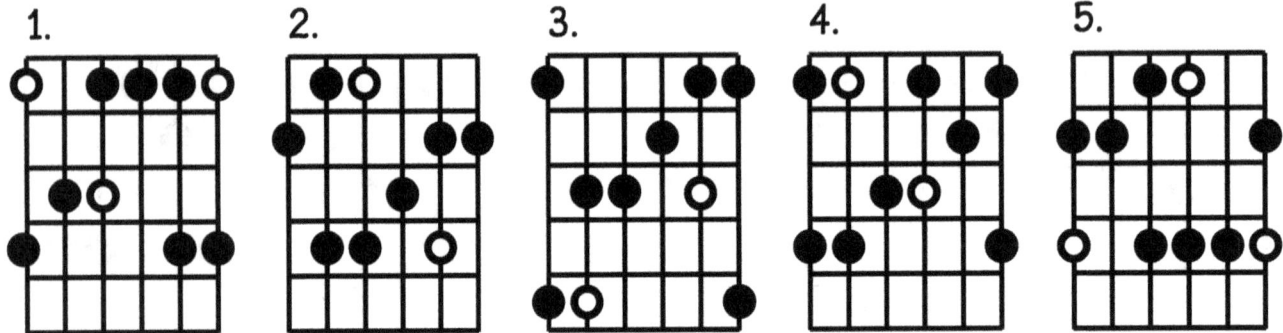

Major 7th

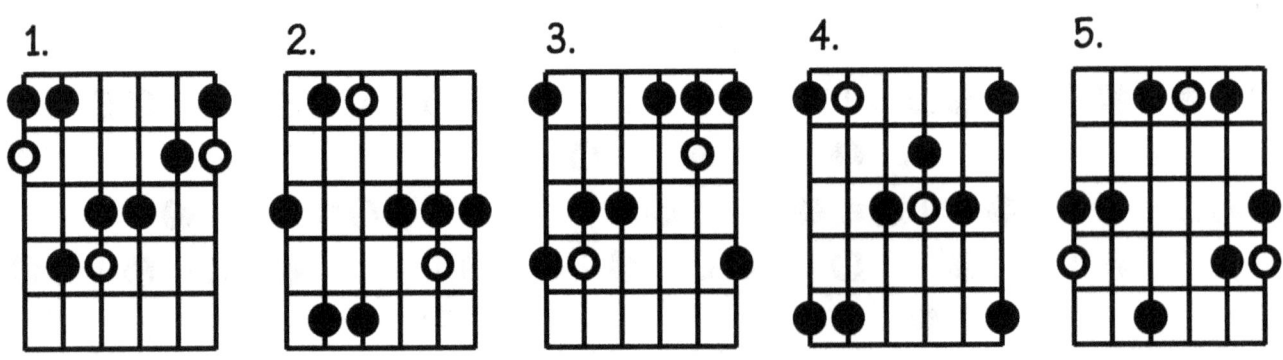

Major Add 9

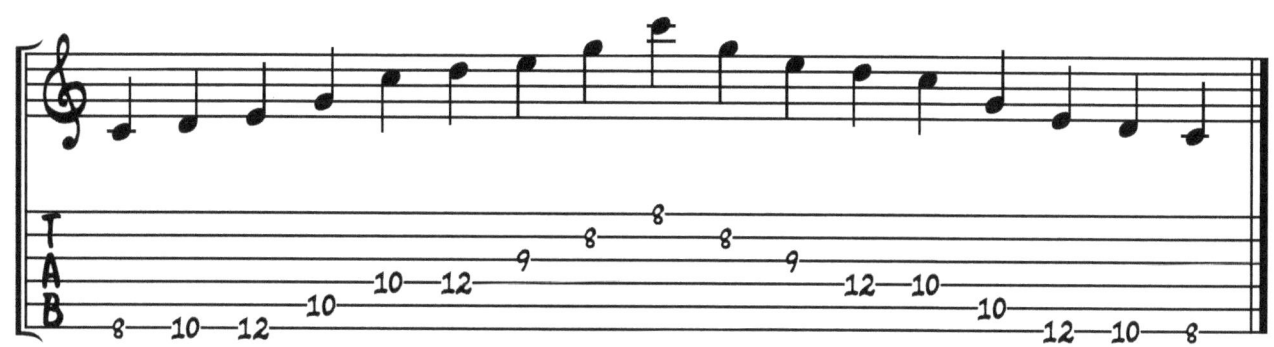

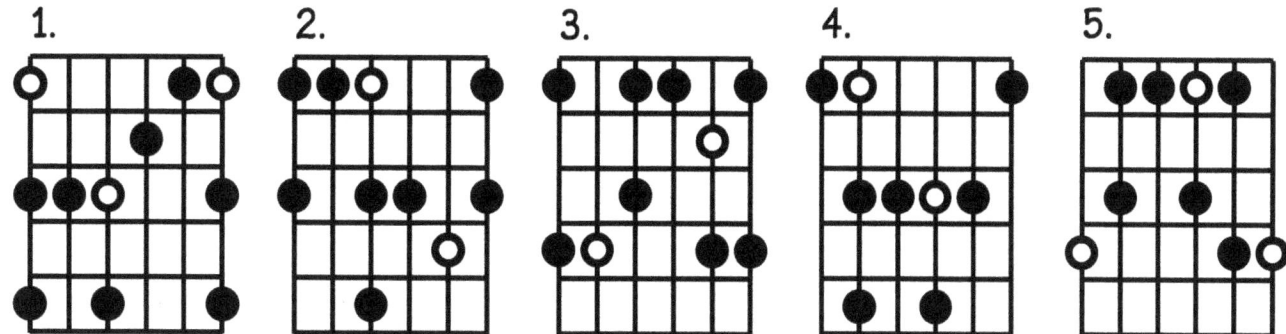

Minor Add 9

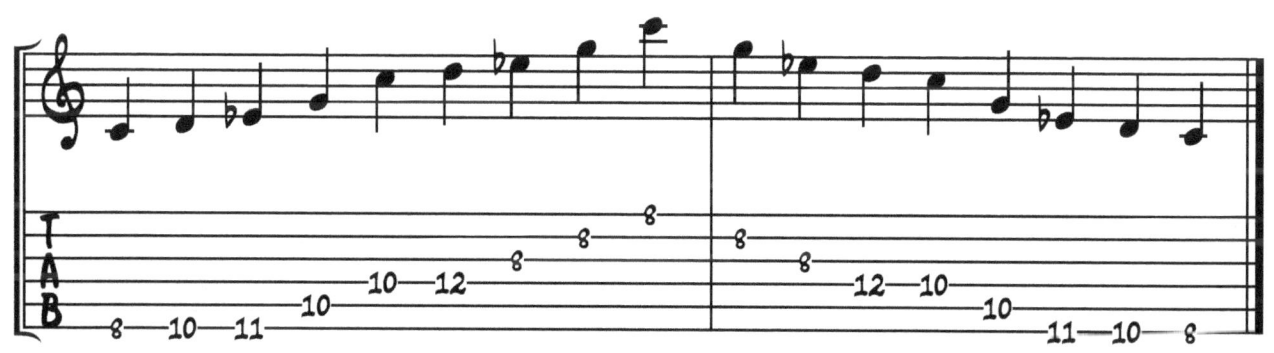

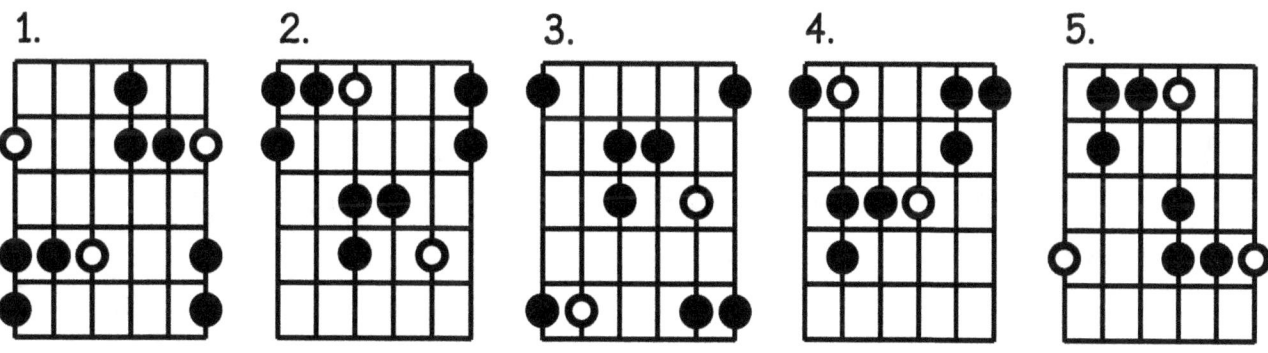

Diminished 7th

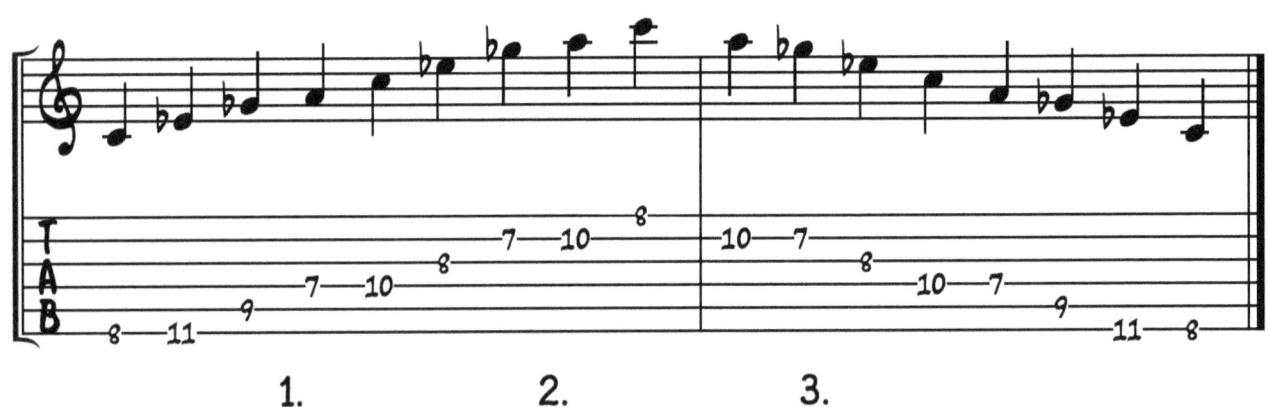

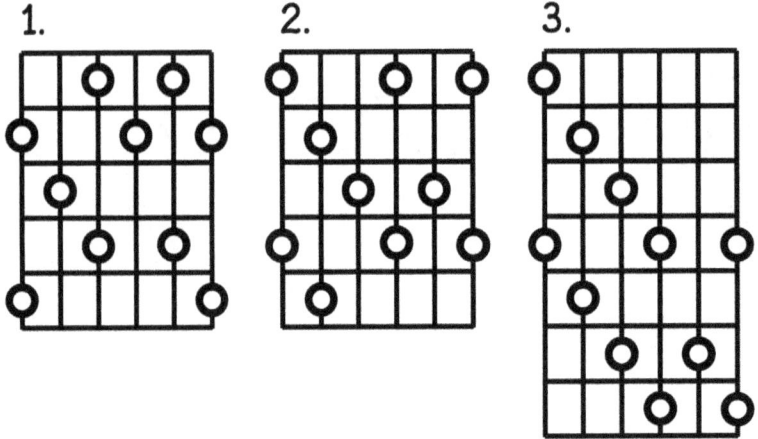

Minor 7th Flat 5

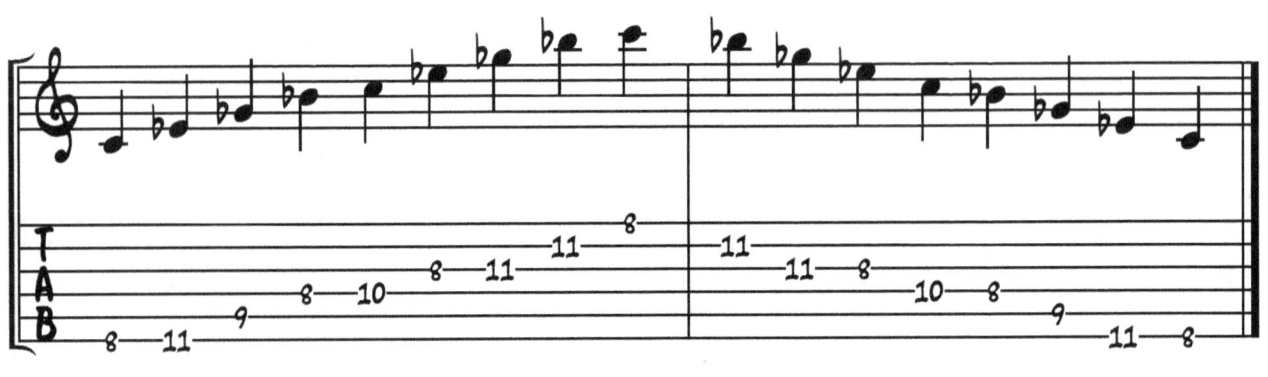

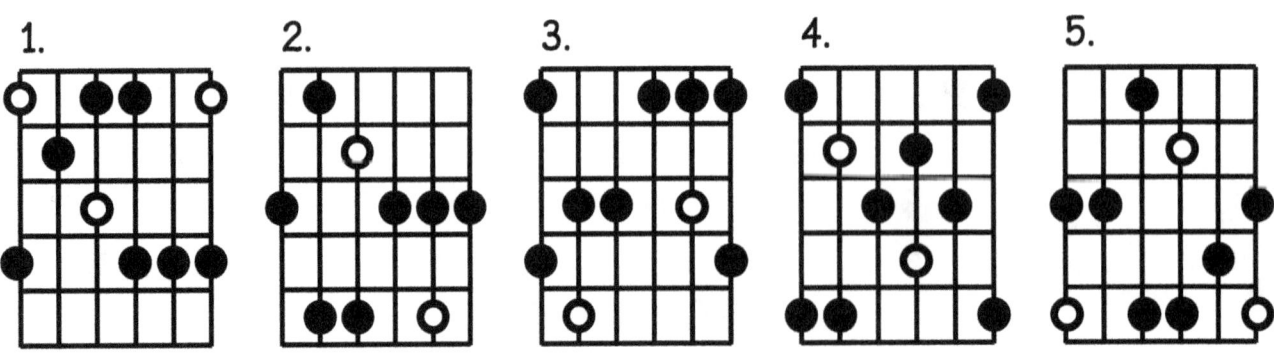

Arpeggios Section 2
Dominant 9th

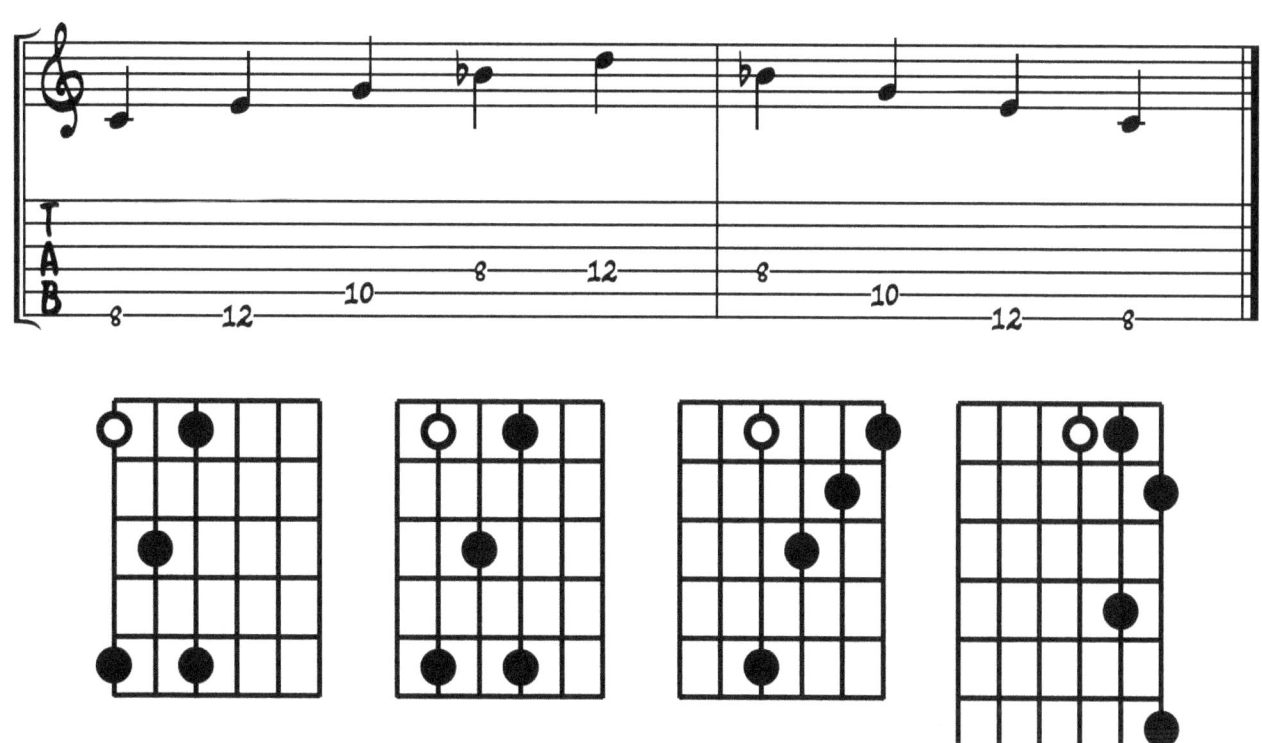

Dominant 11th

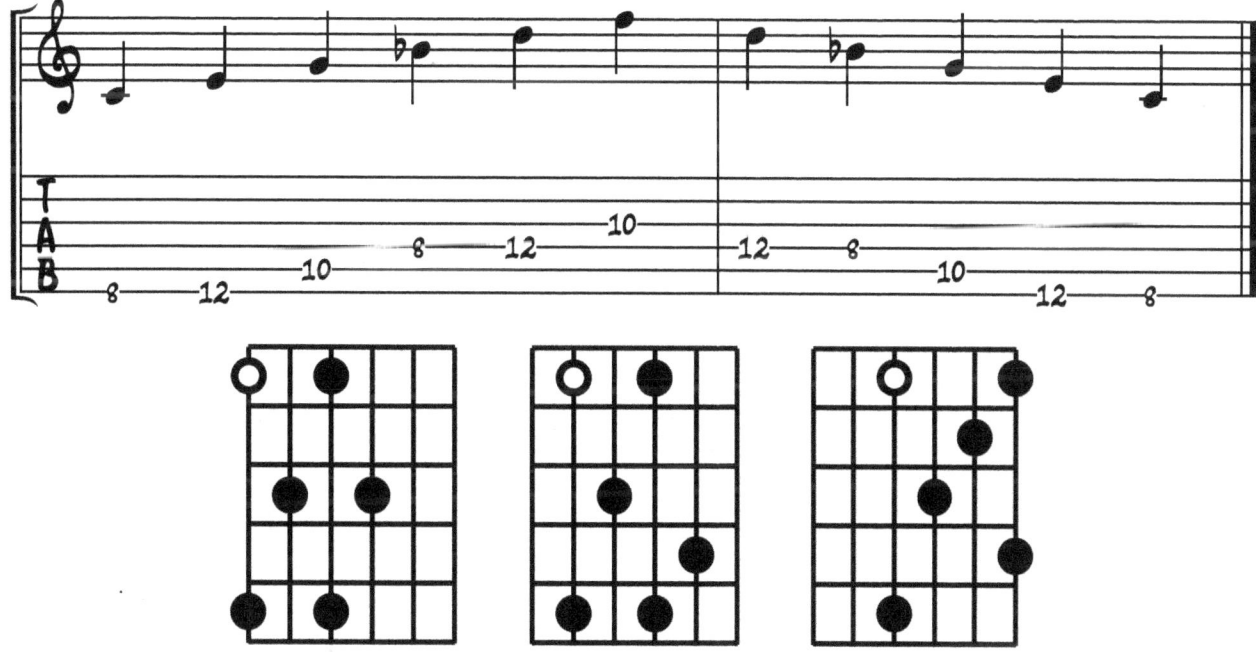

Dominant 13th

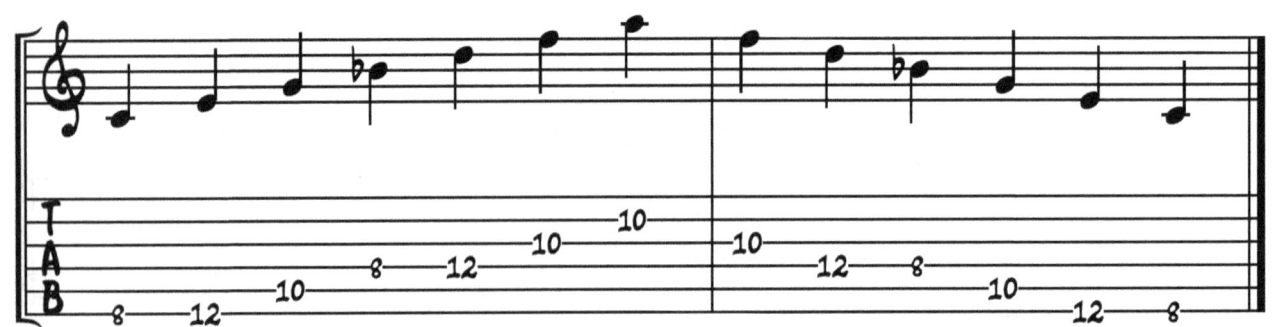

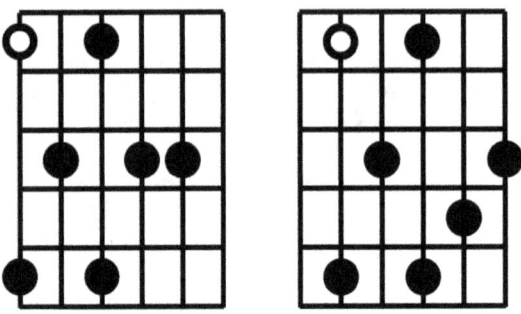

Minor 9th

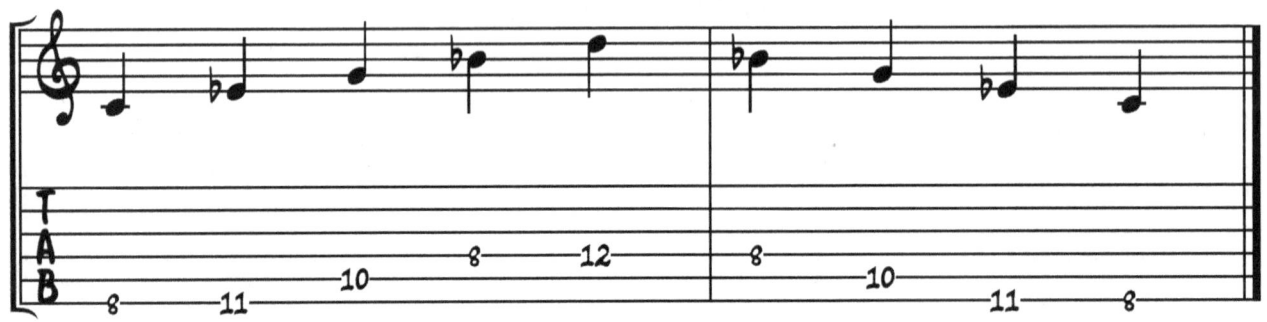

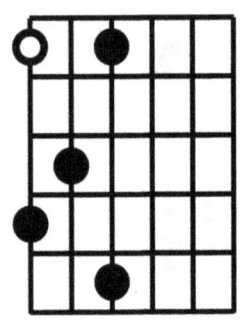 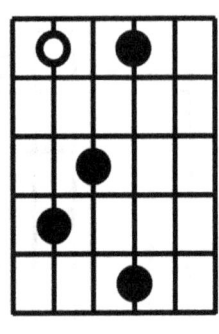 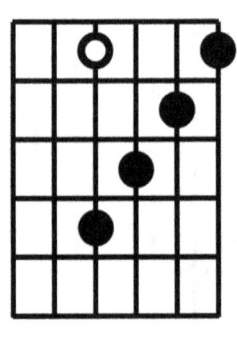 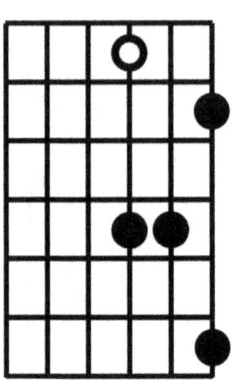

Minor 11th

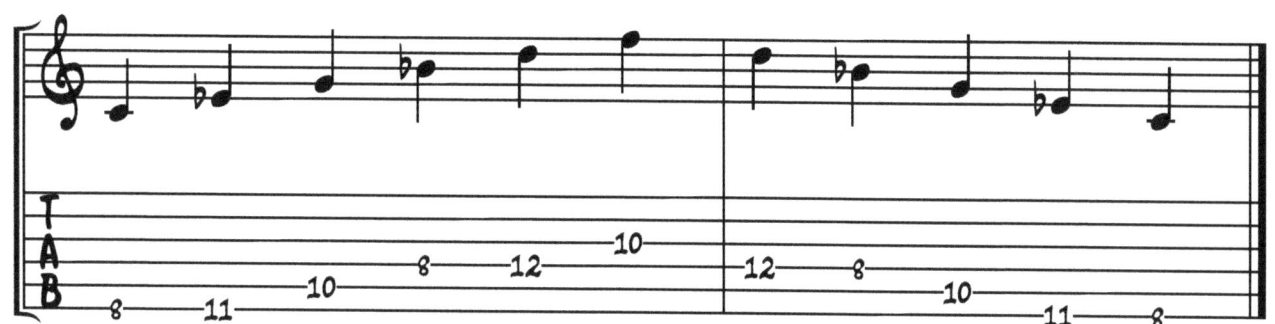

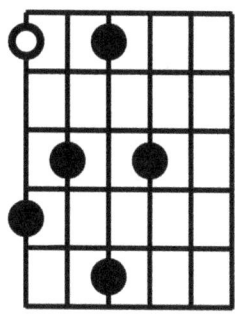 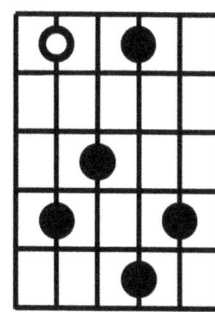 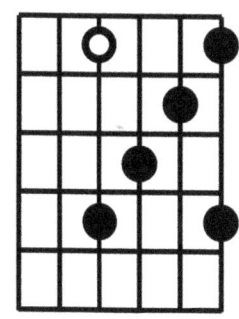

Minor 13th

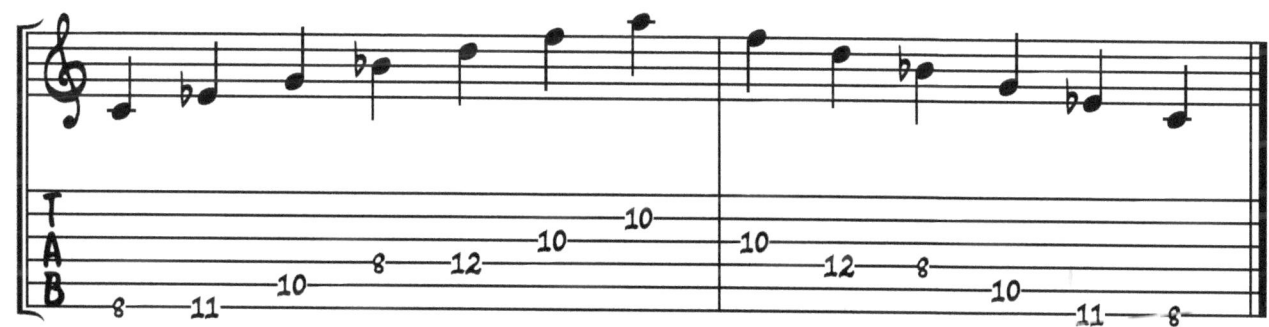

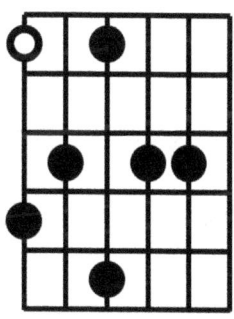 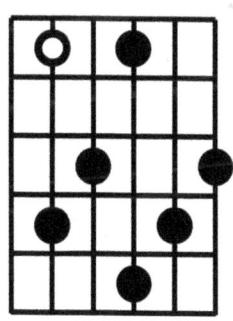

Guitar Command Backing Tracks

Improve Your Lead Guitar Playing With Scales And Modes

You're the lead guitarist.

After the second chorus you have 16 bars to make the song your own.

Is your guitar solo going to be dull, safe and uninspired, or is it going to be a memorable piece of music in its own right?

Break away from the crowd and go with option 2. Use your knowledge of the fretboard to create solos that your fans will love.

Download Guitar Command Backing Tracks from Amazon, iTunes, and many other stores.

Guitar Scales and **Guitar Modes** backing tracks albums have been specially produced for lead guitarists wishing to learn, and practice playing with, scales and modes.

Each track has been written to allow improvisation with a specific scale.

• Learn the scales and modes, then turn them into great music

• Master playing different scales all over the neck and add depth to your solos

Guitar Command Backing Tracks allow you to make the most of your practice time, giving you the advantage you need to stand out from the crowd.

Check out these other awesome backing tracks albums:

Make your solo the highlight of the song.

www.ingramcontent.com/pod-product-compliance
Lightning Source LLC
Chambersburg PA
CBHW081331040426
42453CB00013B/2378